Zawadzki · Lindsay · Cunniffe

ETERNAL

 Published By Black Mask Studios LLC
Matt Pizzolo | Brett Gurewitz | Steve Niles

For this edition, production assistance PHIL SMITH
Produced by MATT PIZZOLO

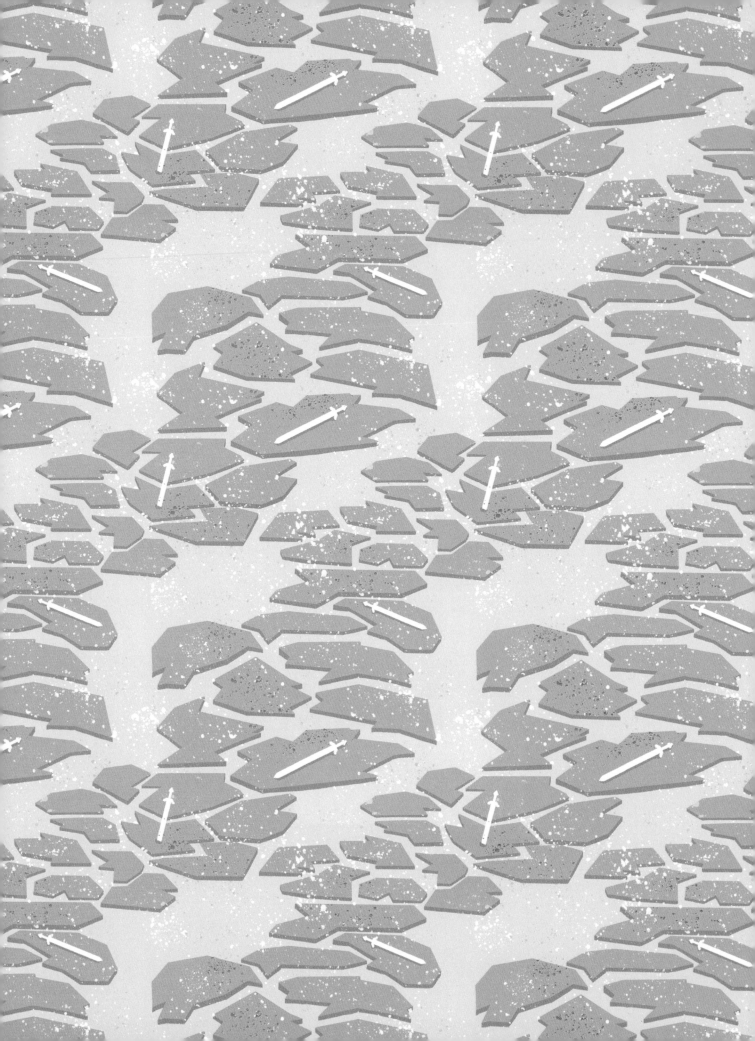

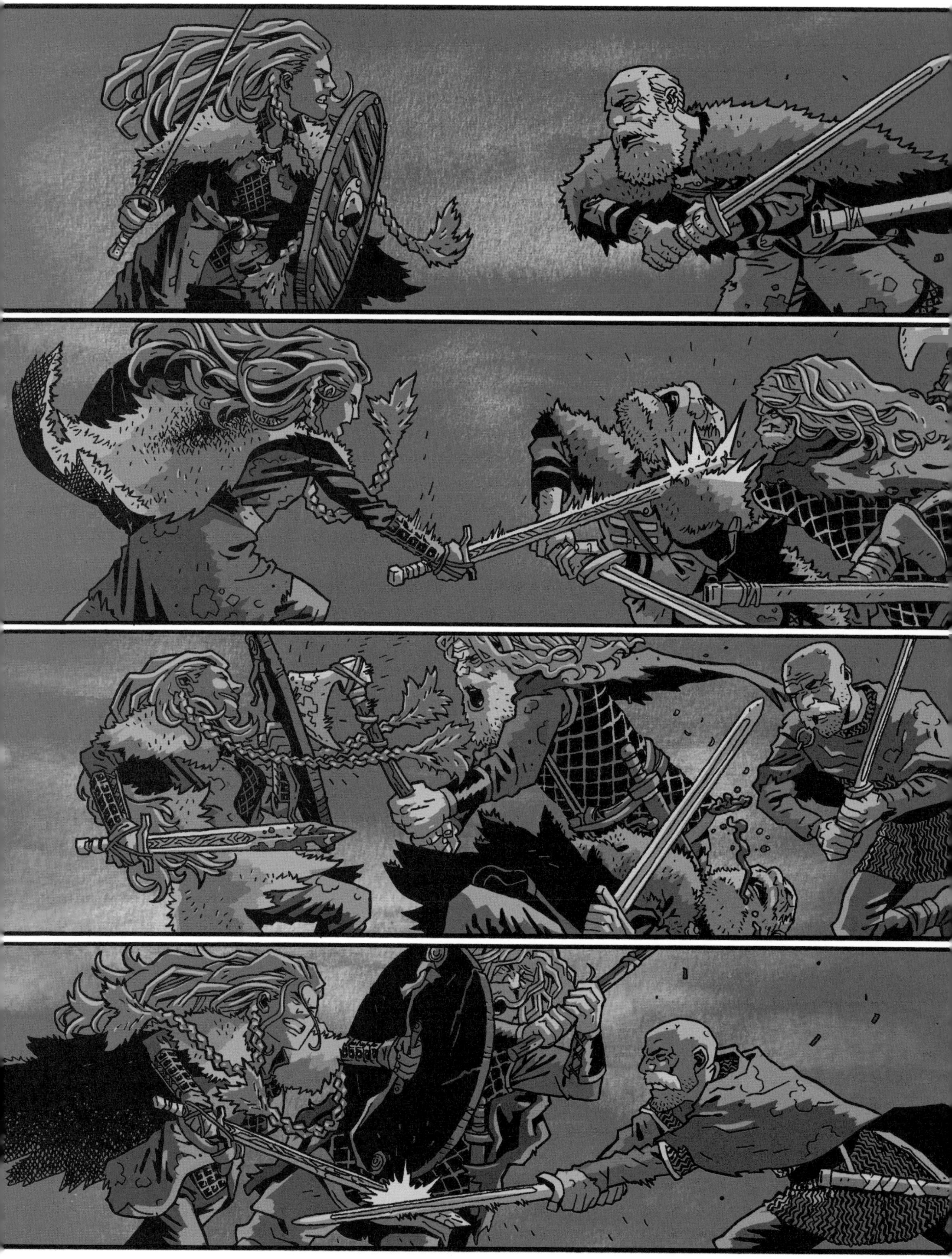

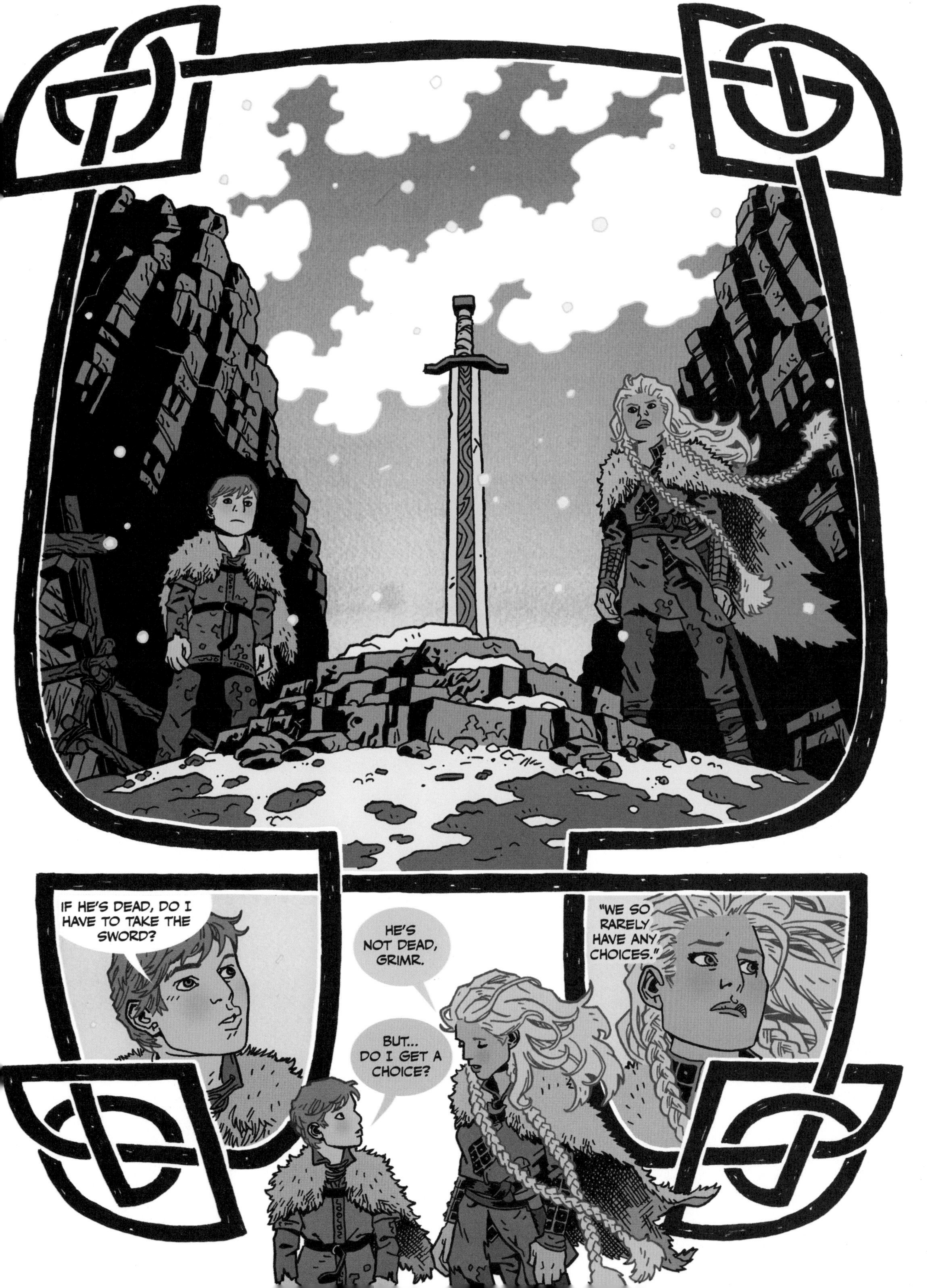
IF HE'S DEAD, DO I HAVE TO TAKE THE SWORD?
HE'S NOT DEAD, GRIMR.
BUT... DO I GET A CHOICE?
"WE SO RARELY HAVE ANY CHOICES."

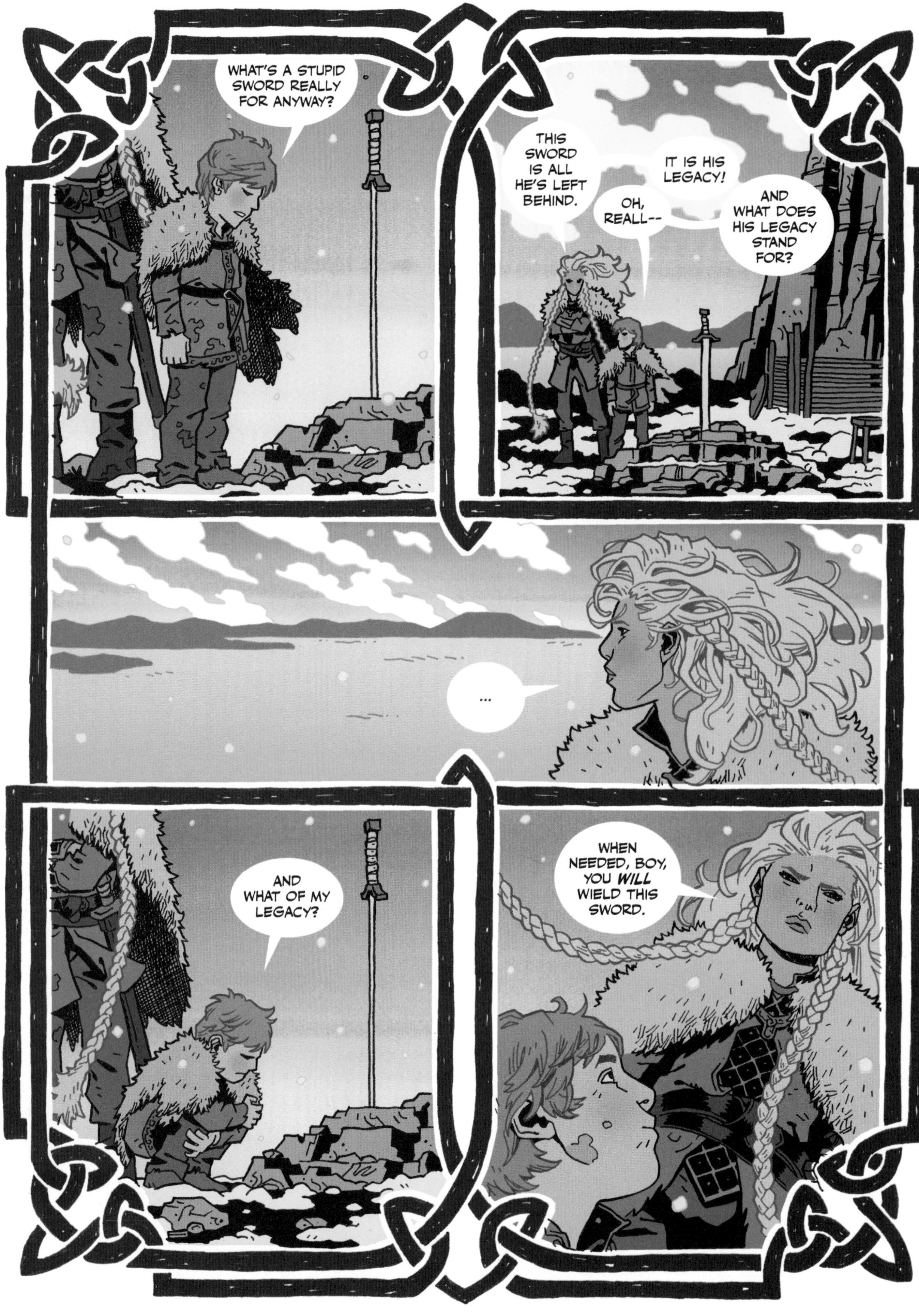
WHAT'S A STUPID SWORD REALLY FOR ANYWAY?
THIS SWORD IS ALL HE'S LEFT BEHIND.
IT IS HIS LEGACY!
OH, REALL--
AND WHAT DOES HIS LEGACY STAND FOR?
...
AND WHAT OF MY LEGACY?
WHEN NEEDED, BOY, YOU *WILL* WIELD THIS SWORD.

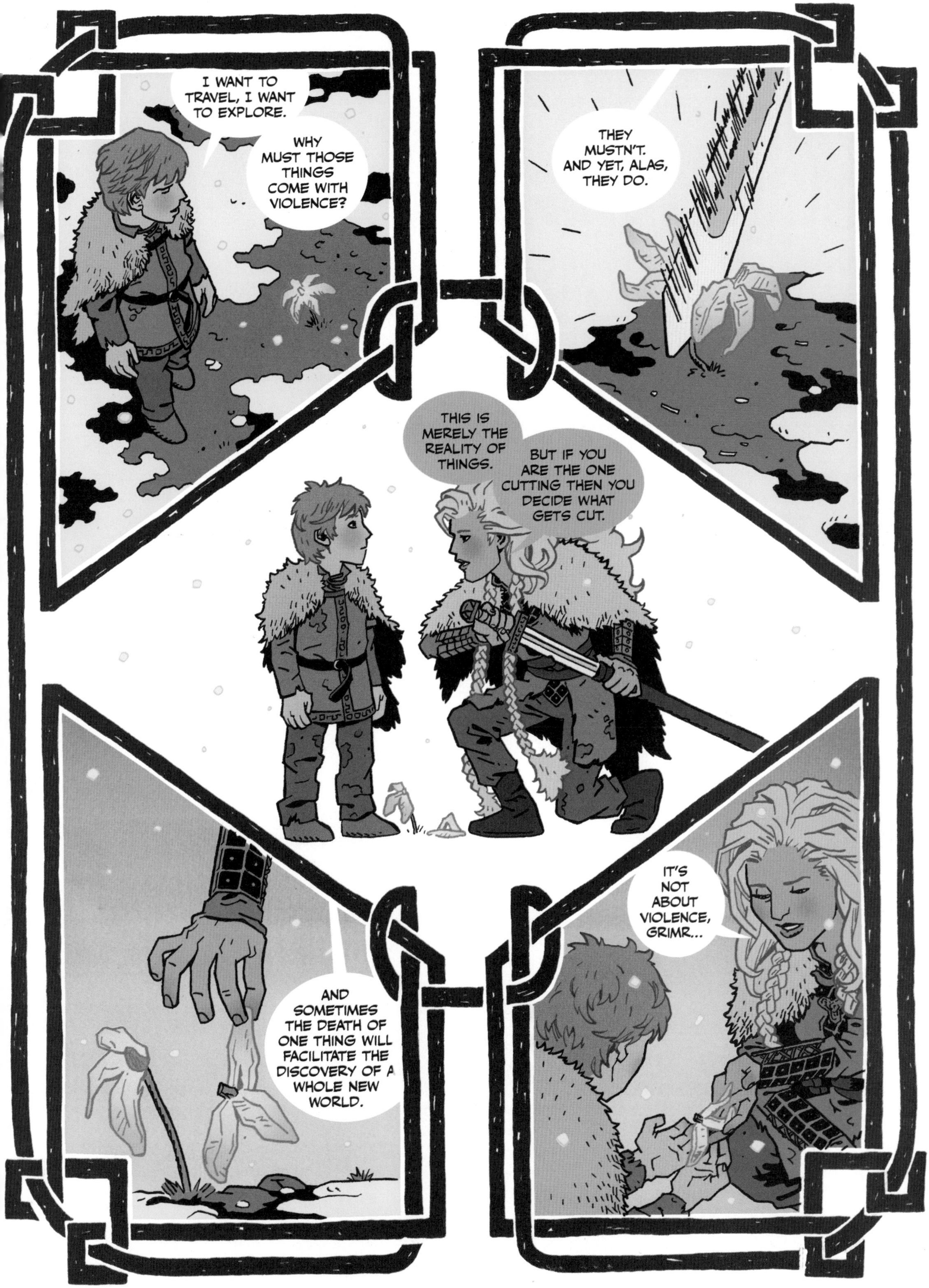
I WANT TO TRAVEL, I WANT TO EXPLORE.
WHY MUST THOSE THINGS COME WITH VIOLENCE?
THEY MUSTN'T. AND YET, ALAS, THEY DO.
THIS IS MERELY THE REALITY OF THINGS.
BUT IF YOU ARE THE ONE CUTTING THEN YOU DECIDE WHAT GETS CUT.
AND SOMETIMES THE DEATH OF ONE THING WILL FACILITATE THE DISCOVERY OF A WHOLE NEW WORLD.
IT'S NOT ABOUT VIOLENCE, GRIMR...

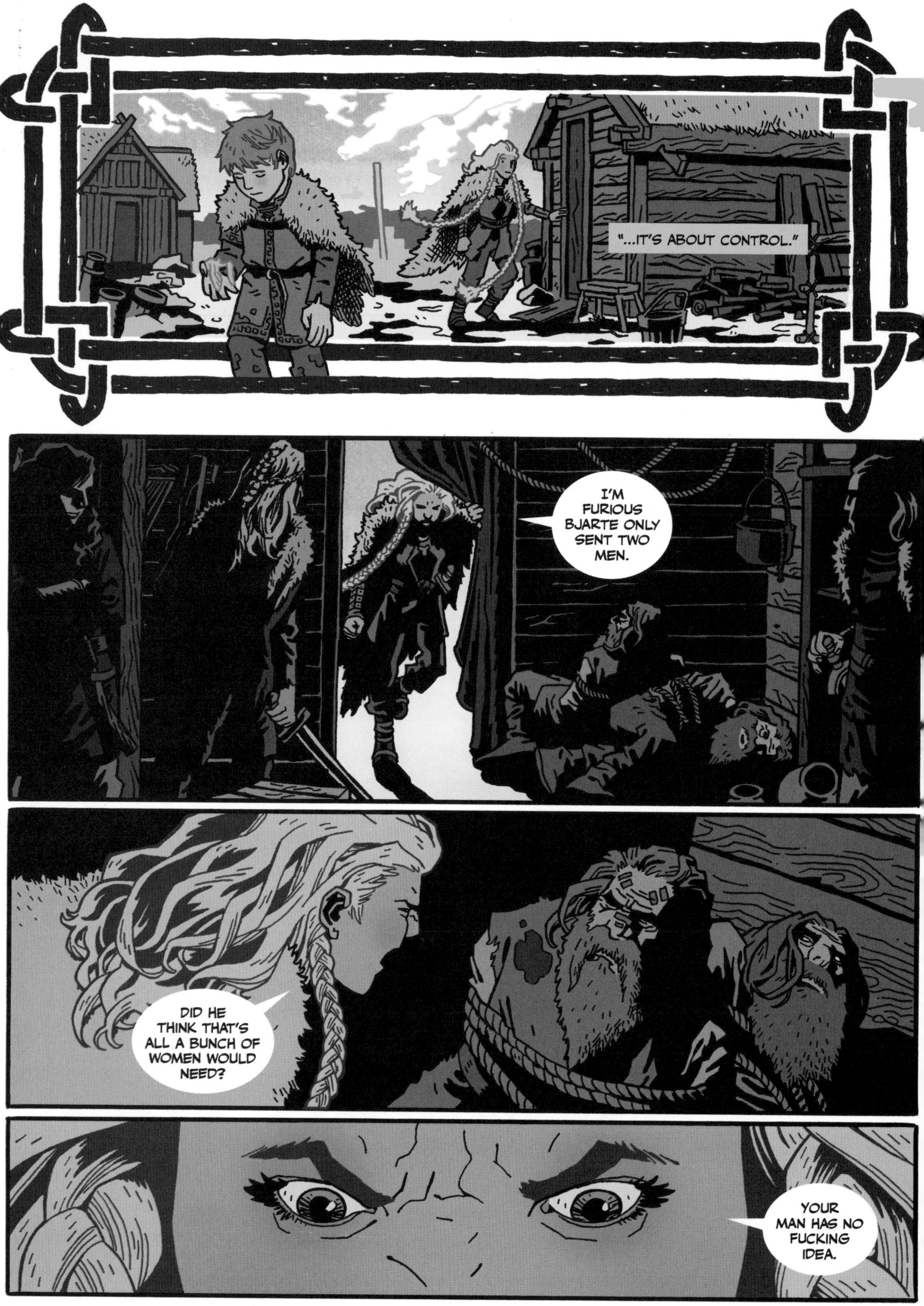
"...IT'S ABOUT CONTROL."
I'M FURIOUS BJARTE ONLY SENT TWO MEN.
DID HE THINK THAT'S ALL A BUNCH OF WOMEN WOULD NEED?
YOUR MAN HAS NO FUCKING IDEA.

ETERNAL
a shieldmaiden ghost story

Story by
Eric Zawadzki & Ryan K Lindsay

Illustrated by
Eric Zawadzki

Colored by
Dee Cunniffe

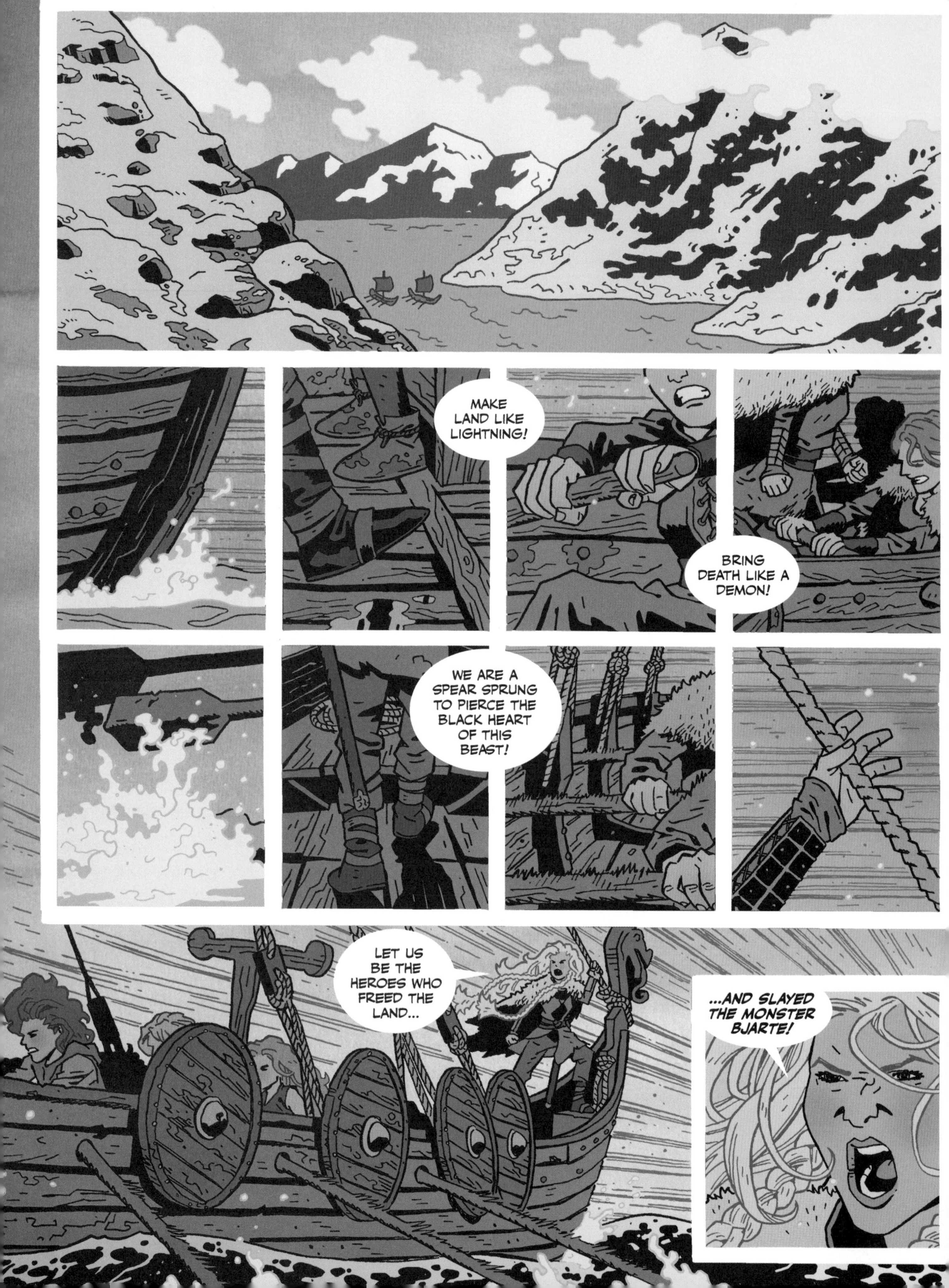
MAKE LAND LIKE LIGHTNING!
BRING DEATH LIKE A DEMON!
WE ARE A SPEAR SPRUNG TO PIERCE THE BLACK HEART OF THIS BEAST!
LET US BE THE HEROES WHO FREED THE LAND...
...AND SLAYED THE MONSTER BJARTE!

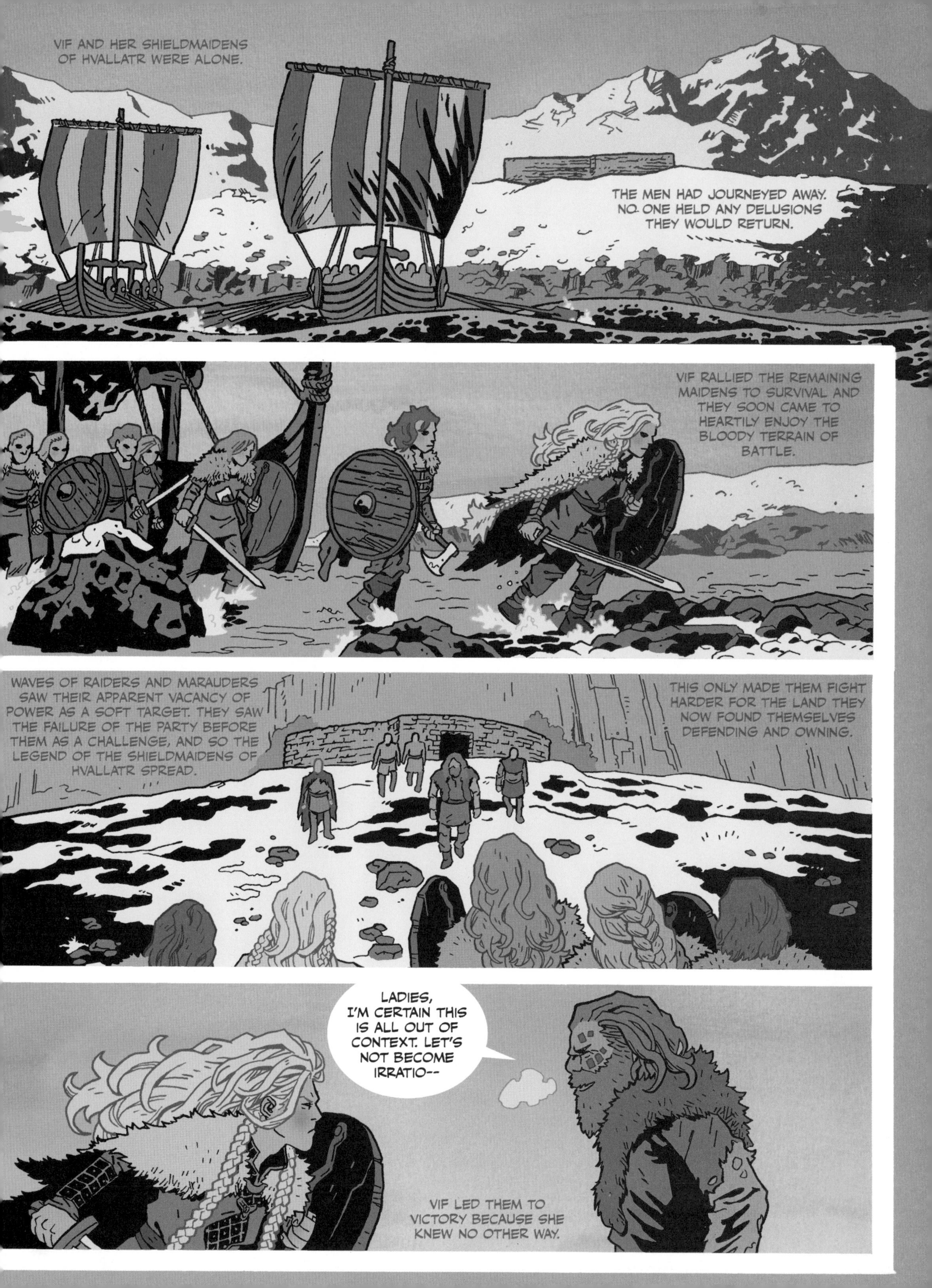
VIF AND HER SHIELDMAIDENS OF HVALLATR WERE ALONE.
THE MEN HAD JOURNEYED AWAY. NO ONE HELD ANY DELUSIONS THEY WOULD RETURN.
VIF RALLIED THE REMAINING MAIDENS TO SURVIVAL AND THEY SOON CAME TO HEARTILY ENJOY THE BLOODY TERRAIN OF BATTLE.
WAVES OF RAIDERS AND MARAUDERS SAW THEIR APPARENT VACANCY OF POWER AS A SOFT TARGET. THEY SAW THE FAILURE OF THE PARTY BEFORE THEM AS A CHALLENGE, AND SO THE LEGEND OF THE SHIELDMAIDENS OF HVALLATR SPREAD.
THIS ONLY MADE THEM FIGHT HARDER FOR THE LAND THEY NOW FOUND THEMSELVES DEFENDING AND OWNING.
LADIES, I'M CERTAIN THIS IS ALL OUT OF CONTEXT. LET'S NOT BECOME IRRATIO--
VIF LED THEM TO VICTORY BECAUSE SHE KNEW NO OTHER WAY.

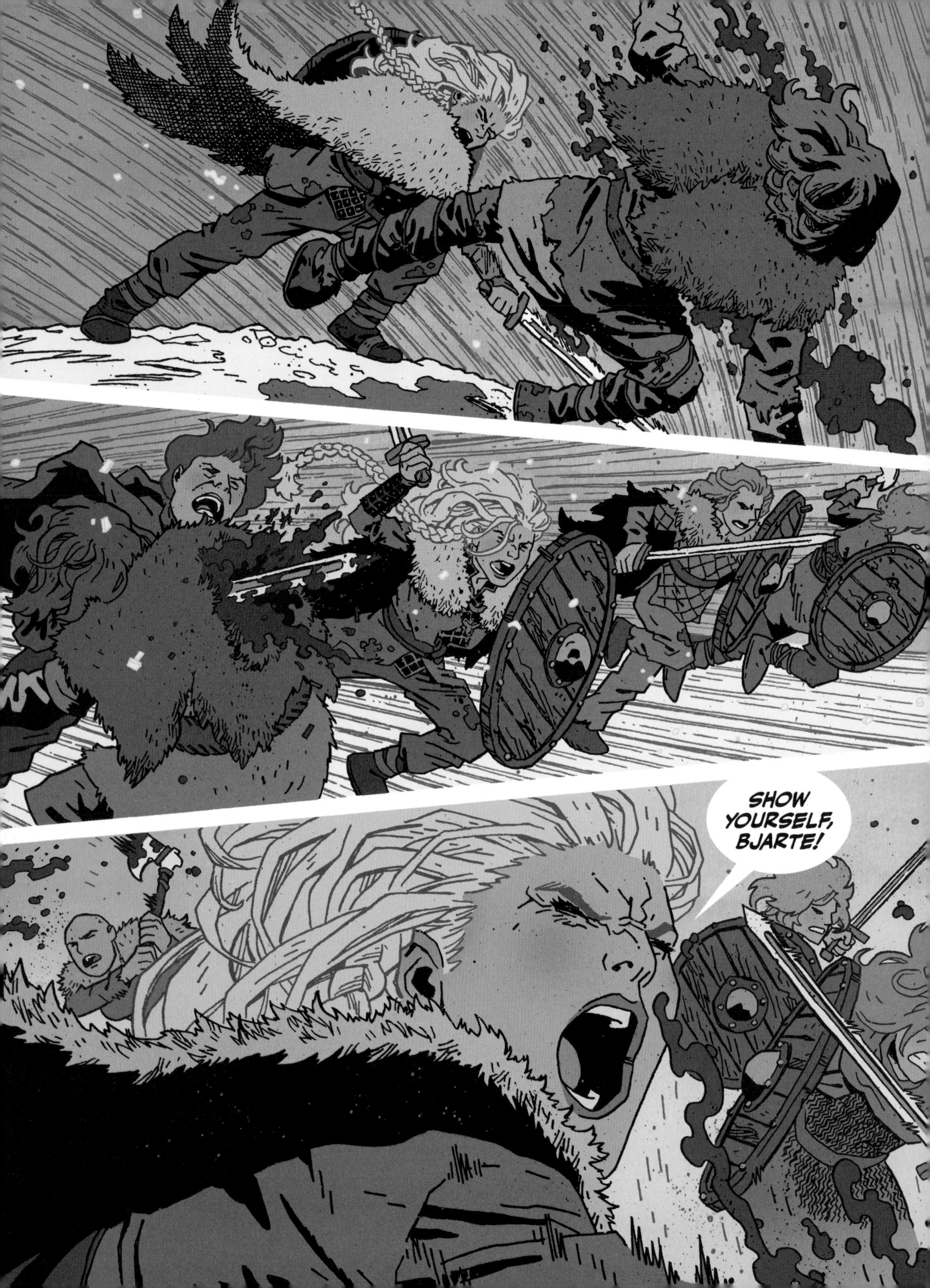
SHOW YOURSELF, BJARTE!

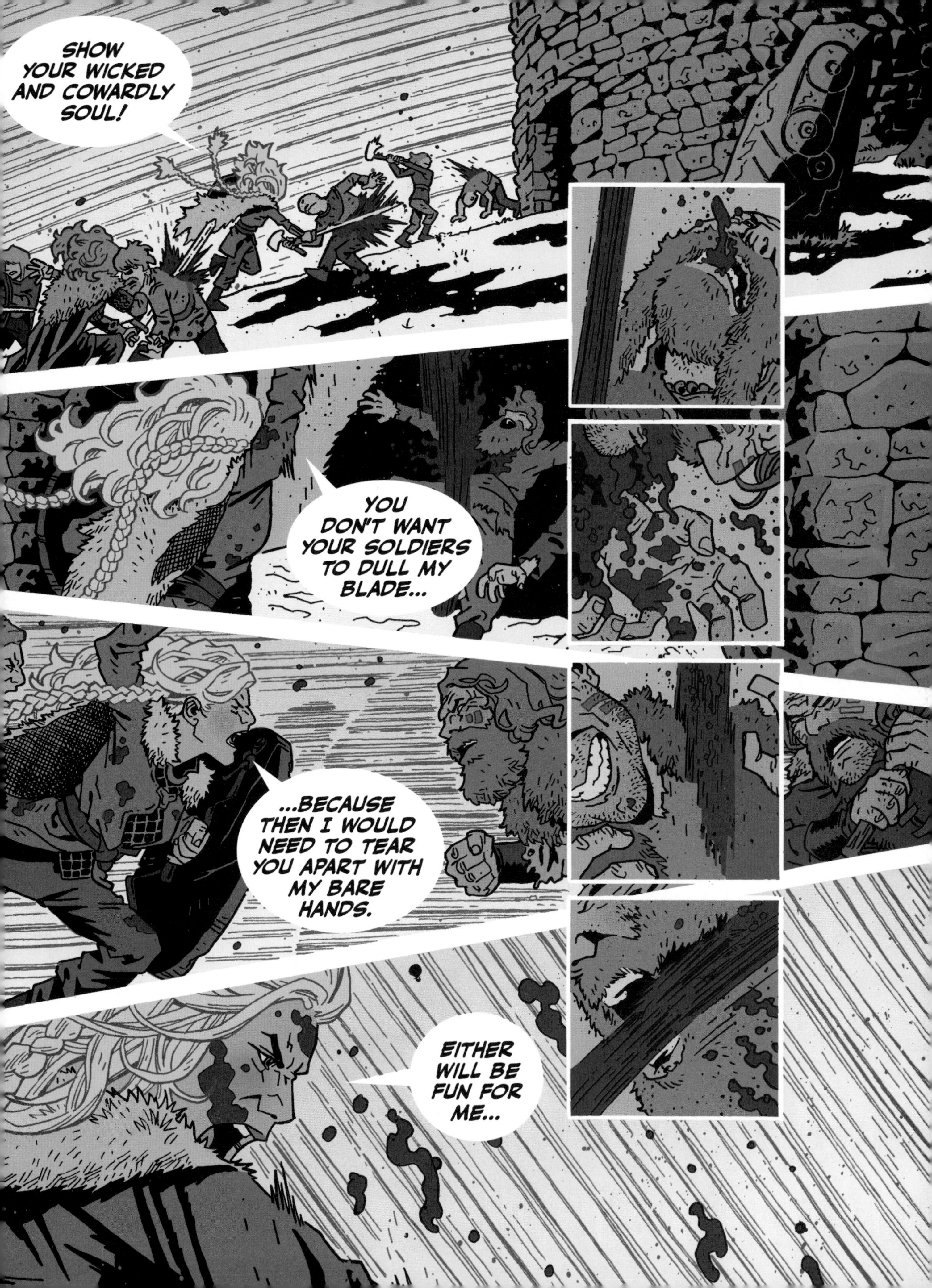
SHOW YOUR WICKED AND COWARDLY SOUL!
YOU DON'T WANT YOUR SOLDIERS TO DULL MY BLADE...
...BECAUSE THEN I WOULD NEED TO TEAR YOU APART WITH MY BARE HANDS.
EITHER WILL BE FUN FOR ME...

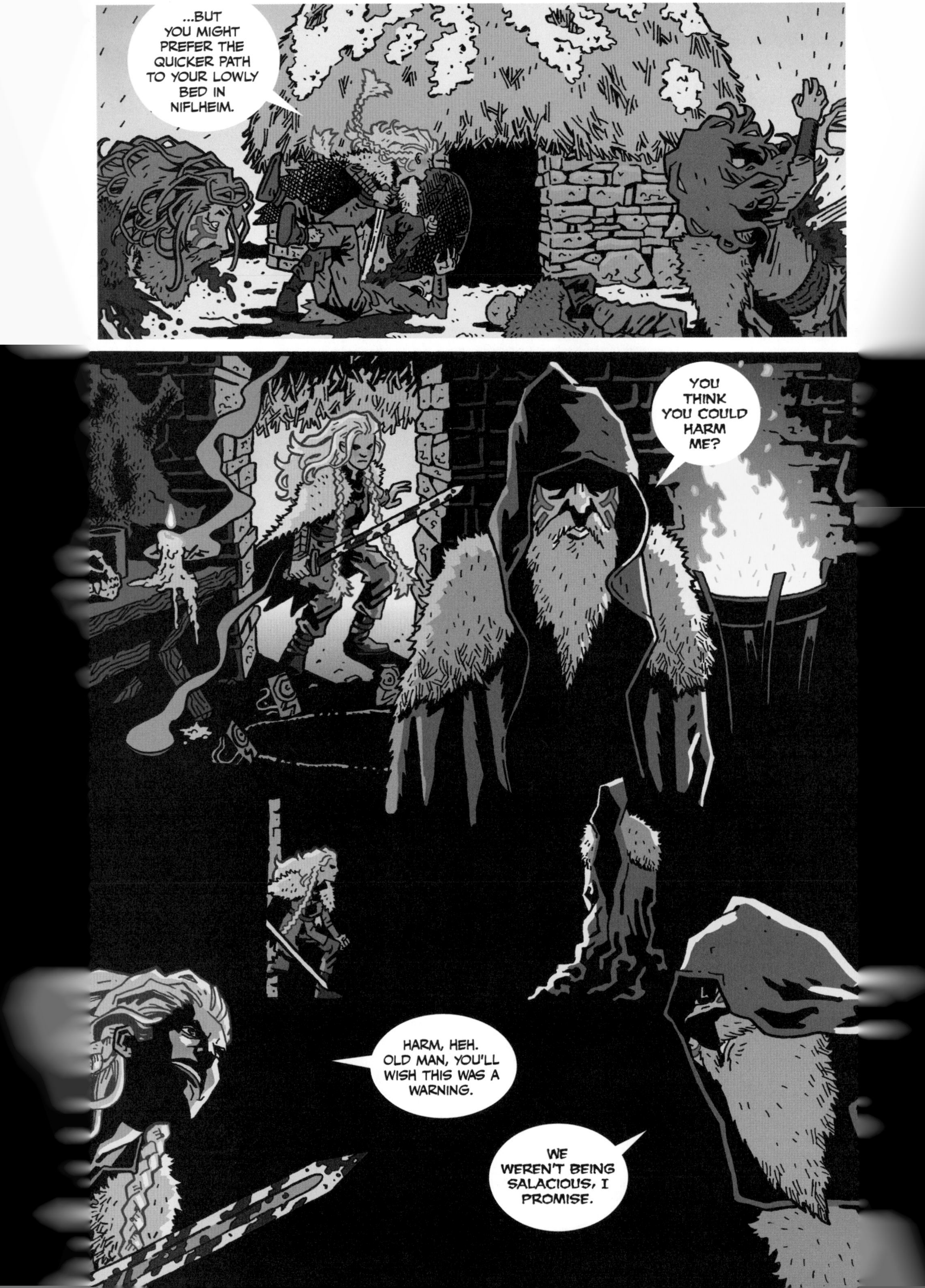
...BUT YOU MIGHT PREFER THE QUICKER PATH TO YOUR LOWLY BED IN NIFLHEIM.
YOU THINK YOU COULD HARM ME?
HARM, HEH. OLD MAN, YOU'LL WISH THIS WAS A WARNING.
WE WEREN'T BEING SALACIOUS, I PROMISE.

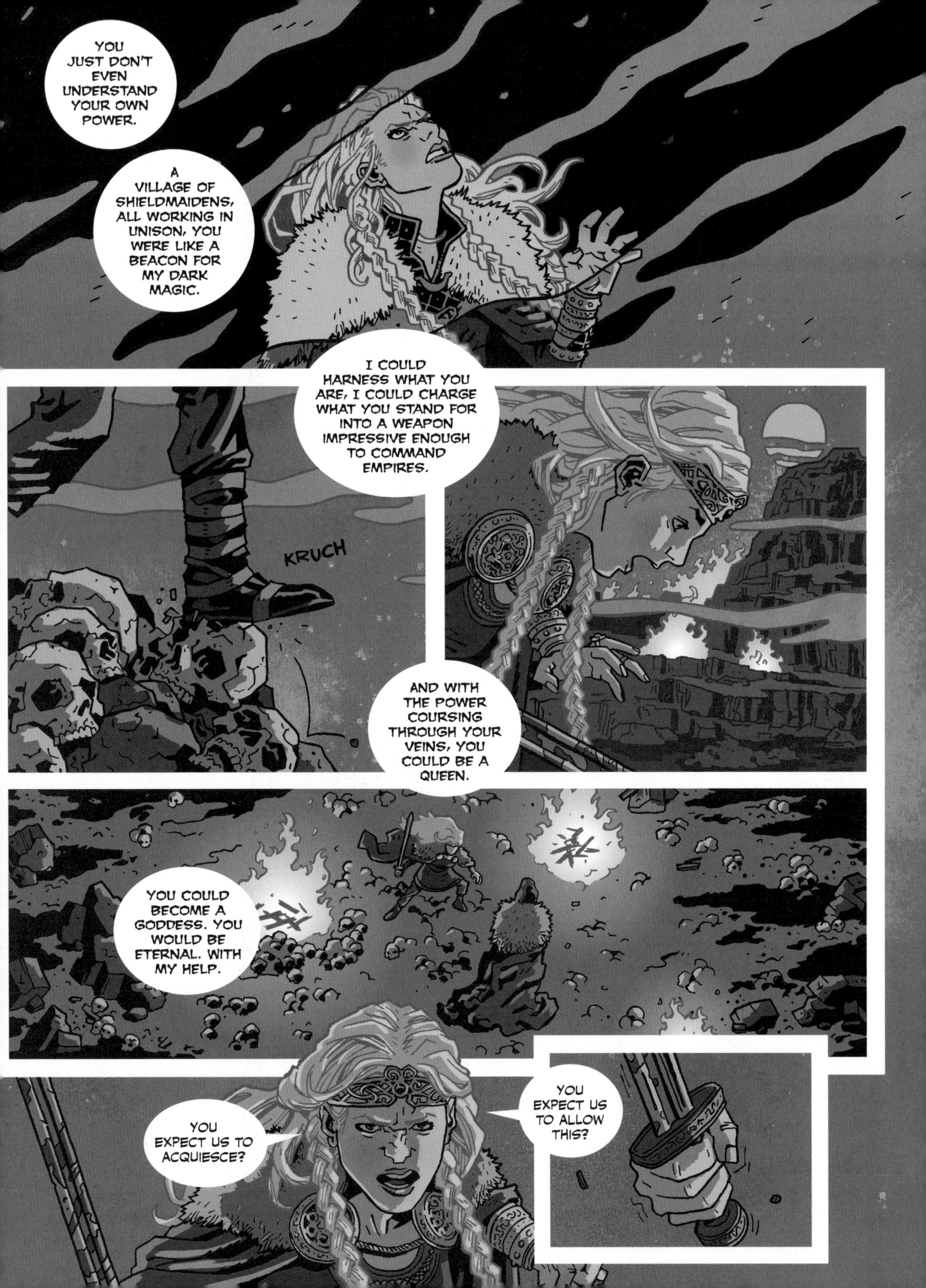
YOU JUST DON'T EVEN UNDERSTAND YOUR OWN POWER.
A VILLAGE OF SHIELDMAIDENS, ALL WORKING IN UNISON, YOU WERE LIKE A BEACON FOR MY DARK MAGIC.
I COULD HARNESS WHAT YOU ARE, I COULD CHARGE WHAT YOU STAND FOR INTO A WEAPON IMPRESSIVE ENOUGH TO COMMAND EMPIRES.
KRUCH
AND WITH THE POWER COURSING THROUGH YOUR VEINS, YOU COULD BE A QUEEN.
YOU COULD BECOME A GODDESS. YOU WOULD BE ETERNAL. WITH MY HELP.
YOU EXPECT US TO ACQUIESCE?
YOU EXPECT US TO ALLOW THIS?

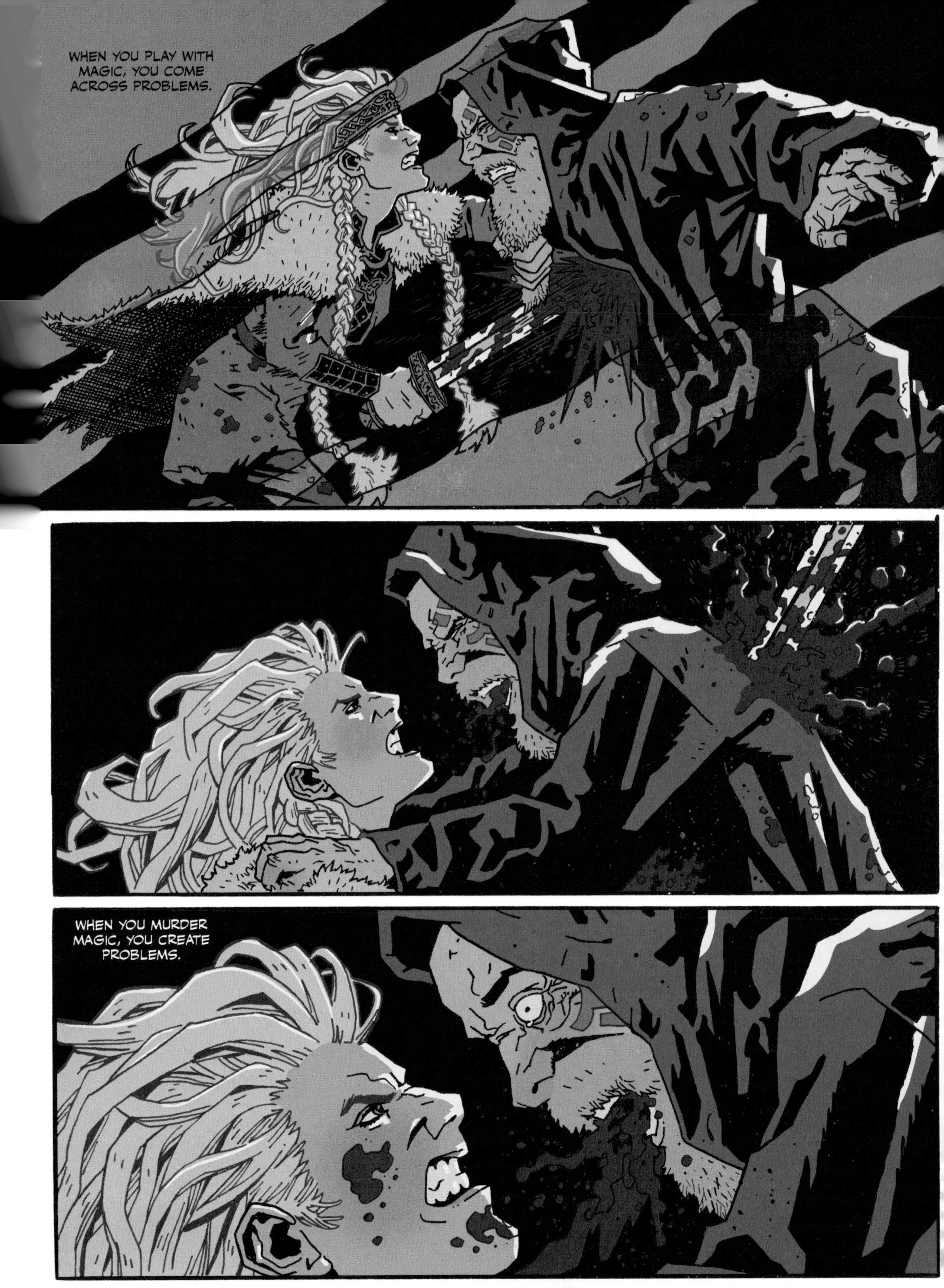
WHEN YOU PLAY WITH MAGIC, YOU COME ACROSS PROBLEMS.
WHEN YOU MURDER MAGIC, YOU CREATE PROBLEMS.

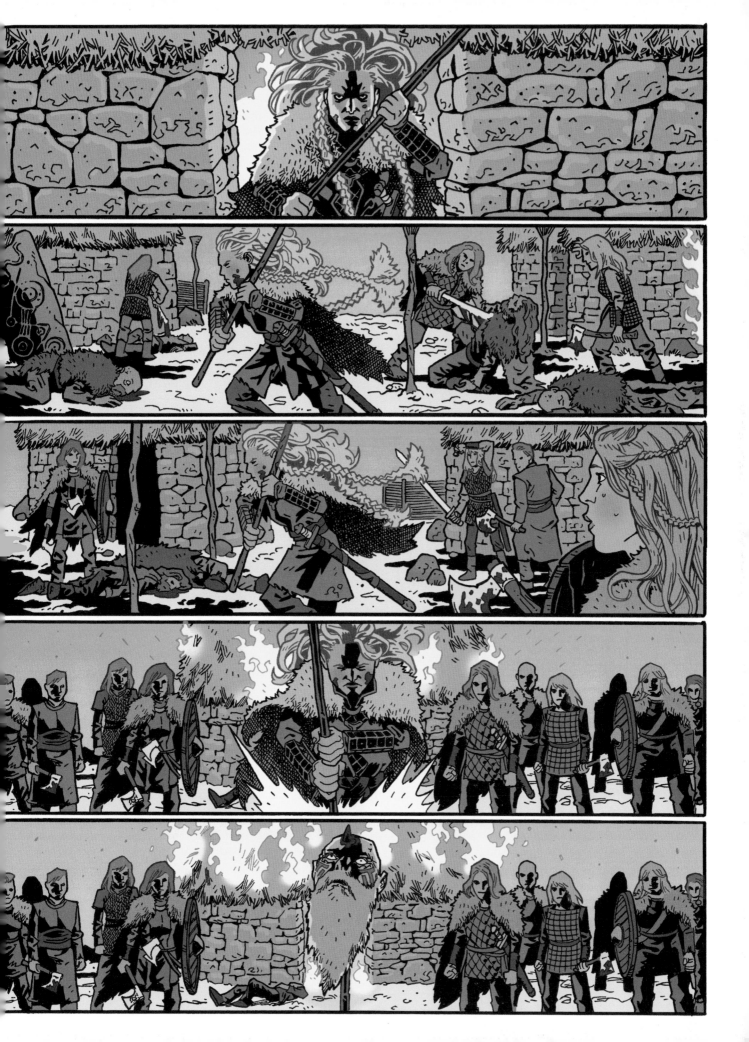

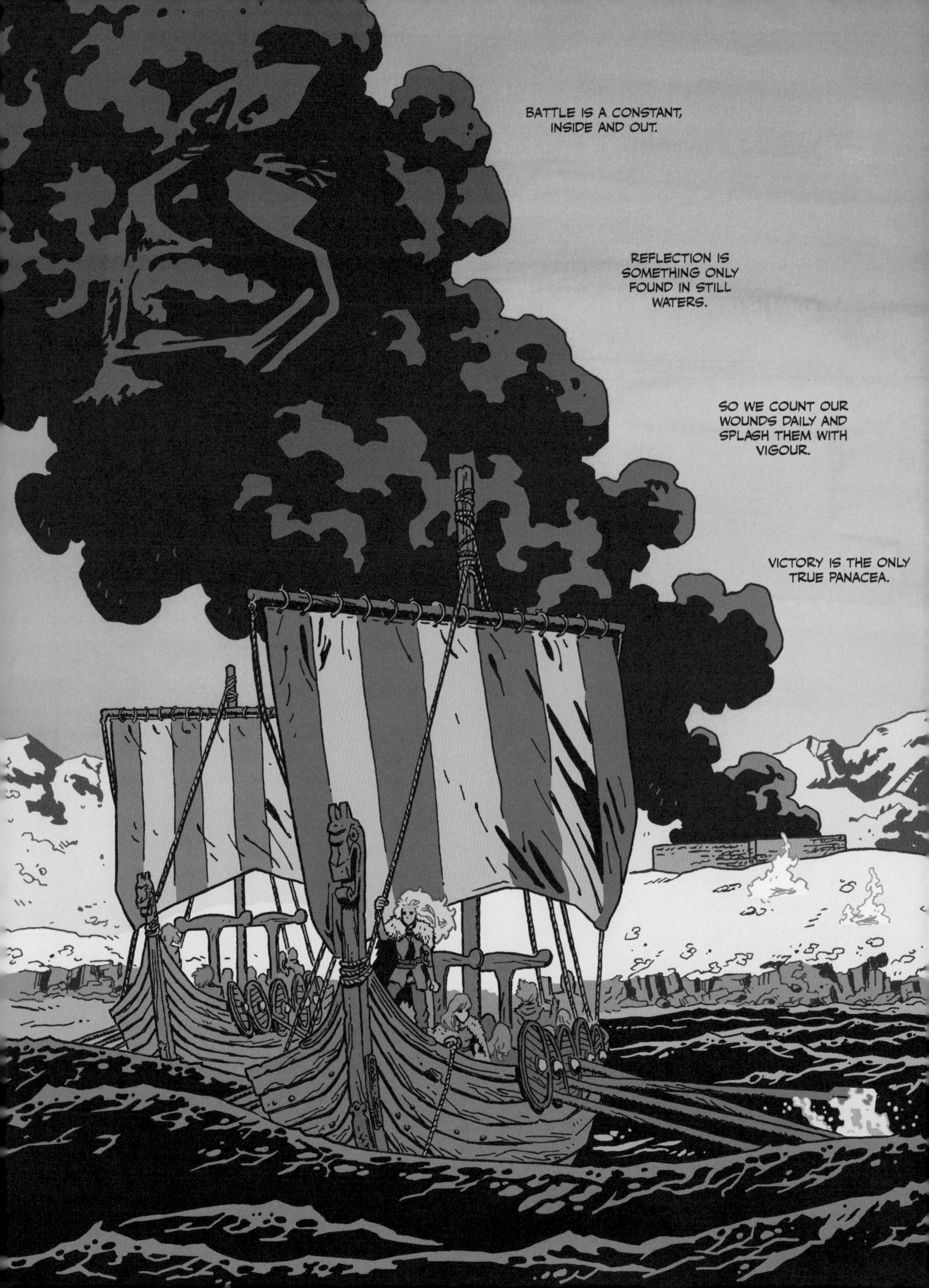
BATTLE IS A CONSTANT, INSIDE AND OUT.
REFLECTION IS SOMETHING ONLY FOUND IN STILL WATERS.
SO WE COUNT OUR WOUNDS DAILY AND SPLASH THEM WITH VIGOUR.
VICTORY IS THE ONLY TRUE PANACEA.

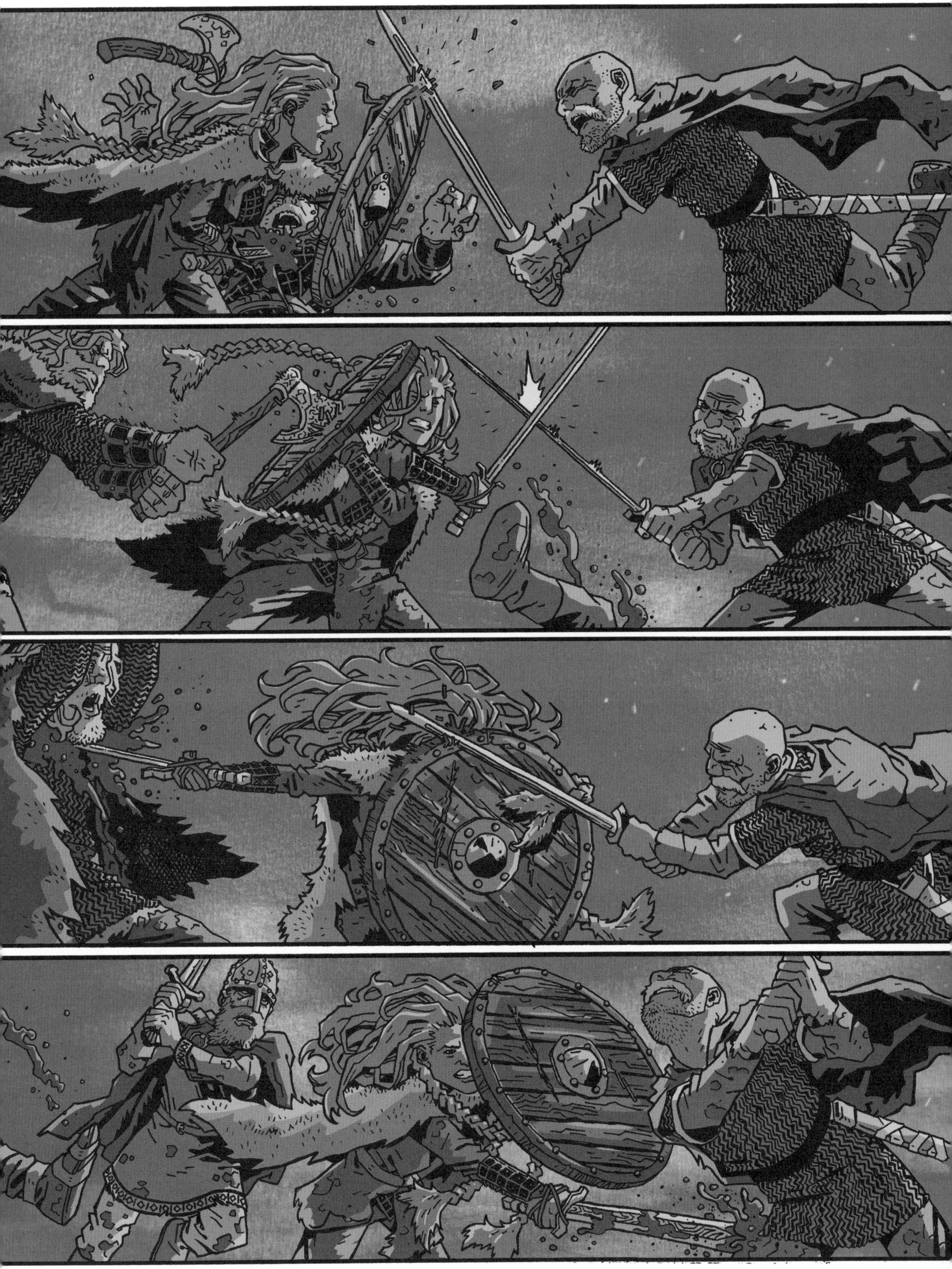

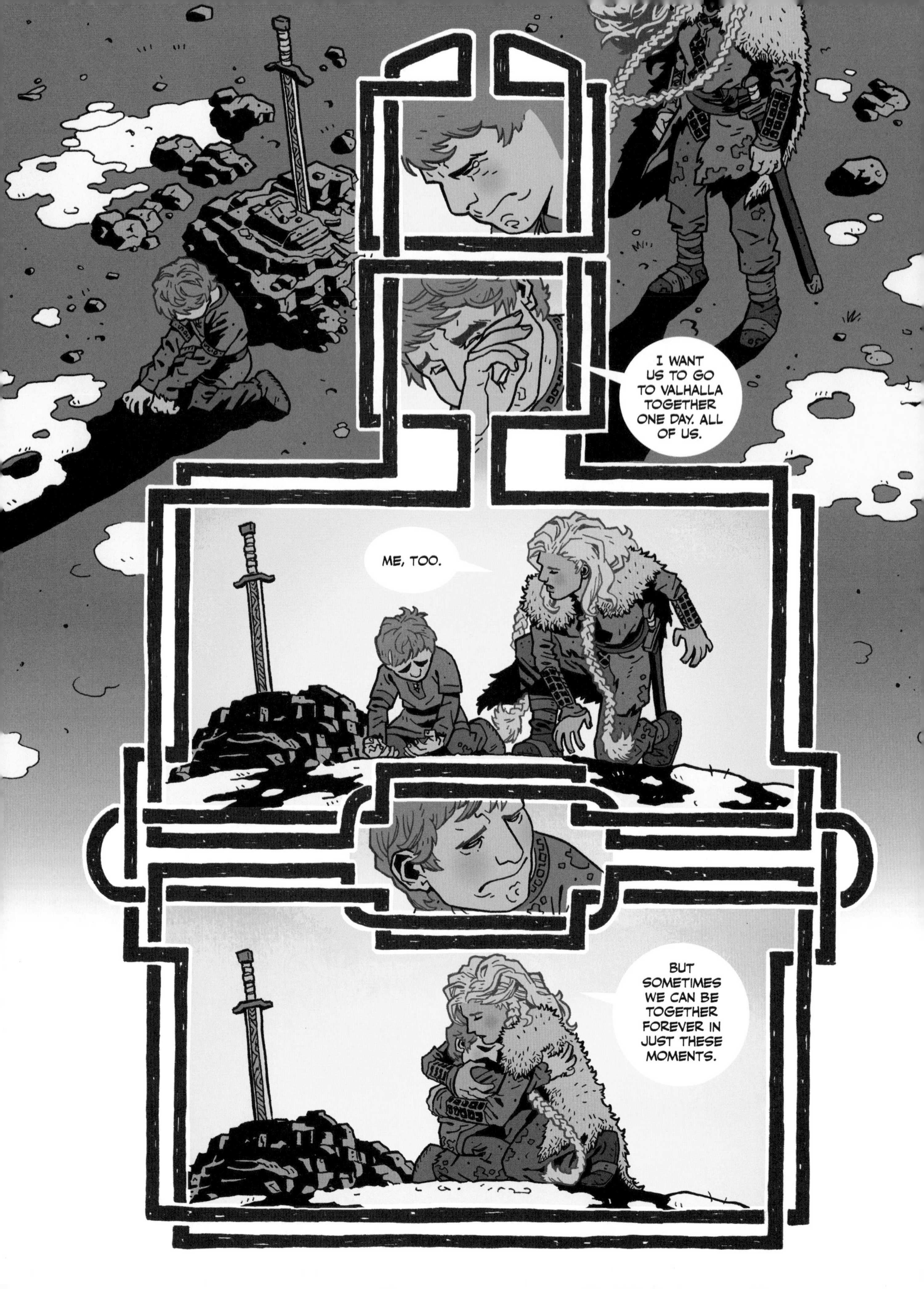
I WANT US TO GO TO VALHALLA TOGETHER ONE DAY. ALL OF US.
ME, TOO.
BUT SOMETIMES WE CAN BE TOGETHER FOREVER IN JUST THESE MOMENTS.

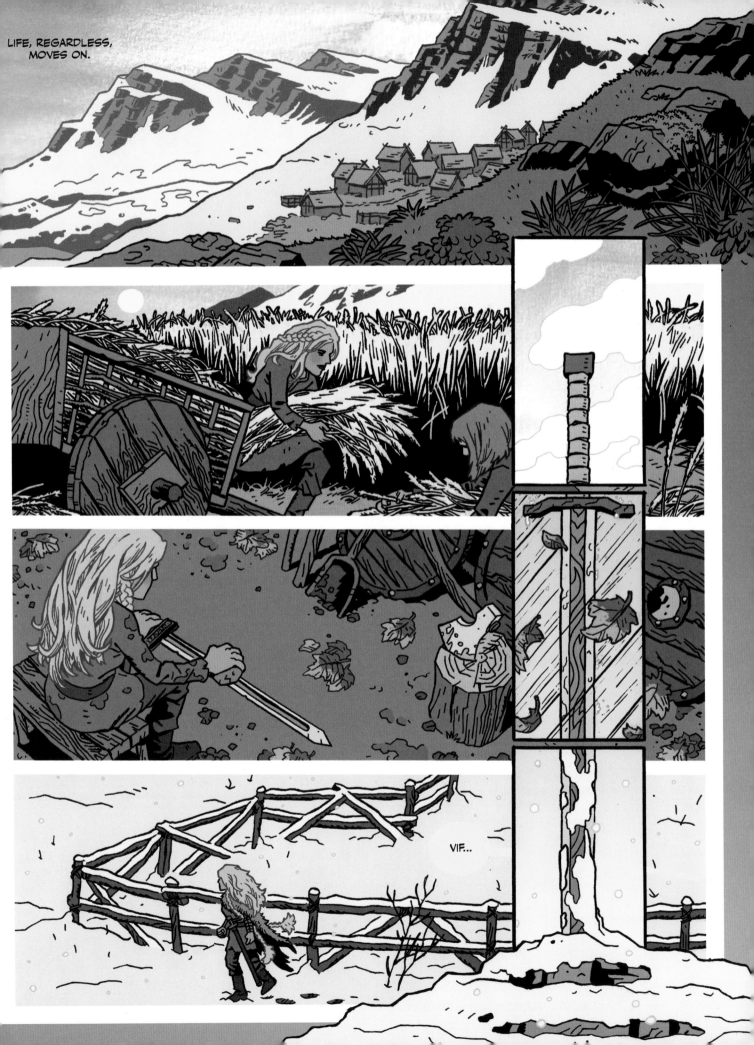

LIFE, REGARDLESS,
MOVES ON.

VIF...

VIF! WE HOLD GRAVE NEWS!

"SOME OF US WERE RETURNING BY WATER AND WE SAW SOMETHING..."

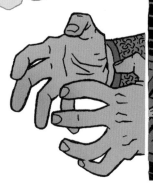

"...UNNATURAL."

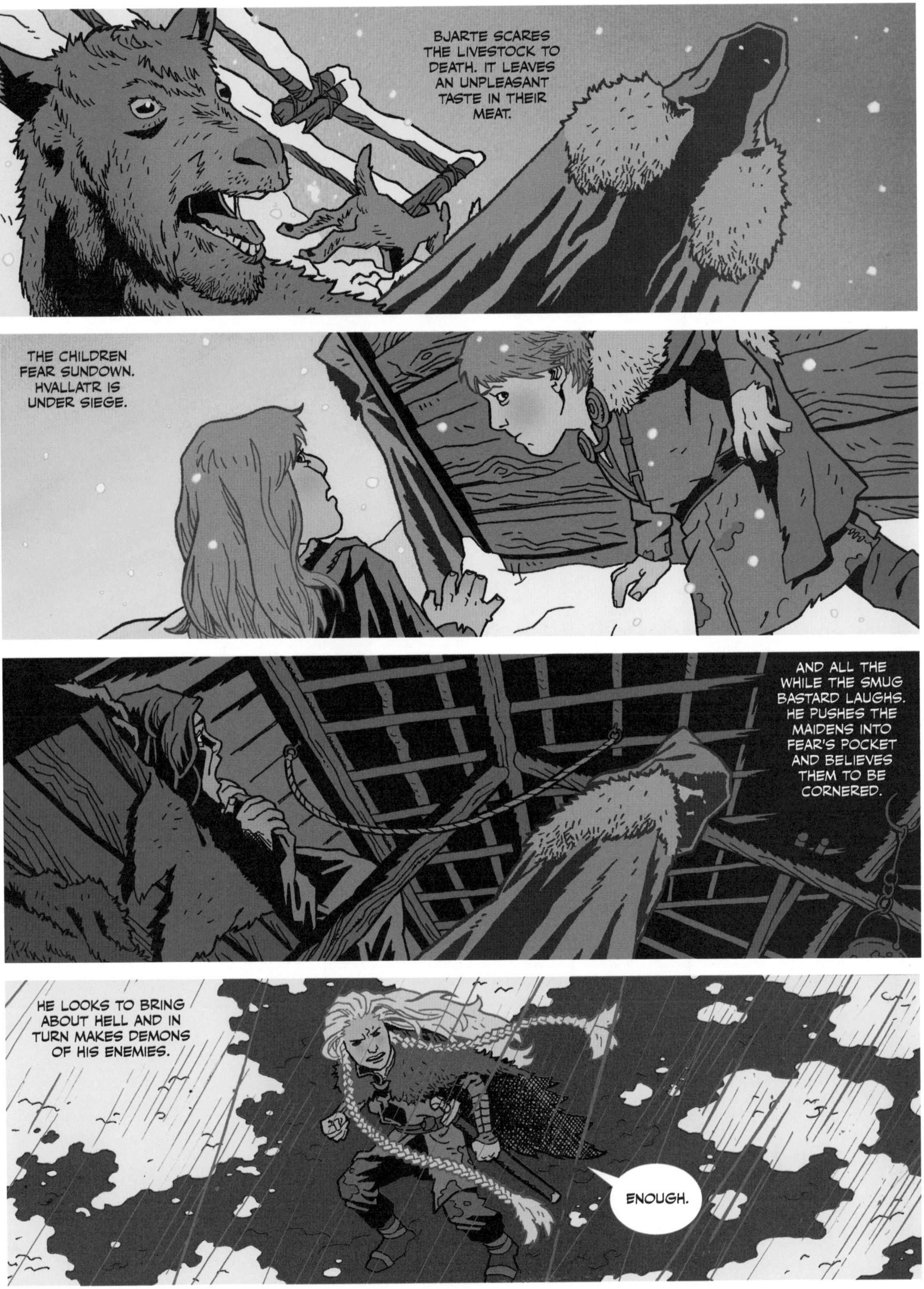
BJARTE SCARES THE LIVESTOCK TO DEATH. IT LEAVES AN UNPLEASANT TASTE IN THEIR MEAT.
THE CHILDREN FEAR SUNDOWN. HVALLATR IS UNDER SIEGE.
AND ALL THE WHILE THE SMUG BASTARD LAUGHS. HE PUSHES THE MAIDENS INTO FEAR'S POCKET AND BELIEVES THEM TO BE CORNERED.
HE LOOKS TO BRING ABOUT HELL AND IN TURN MAKES DEMONS OF HIS ENEMIES.
ENOUGH.

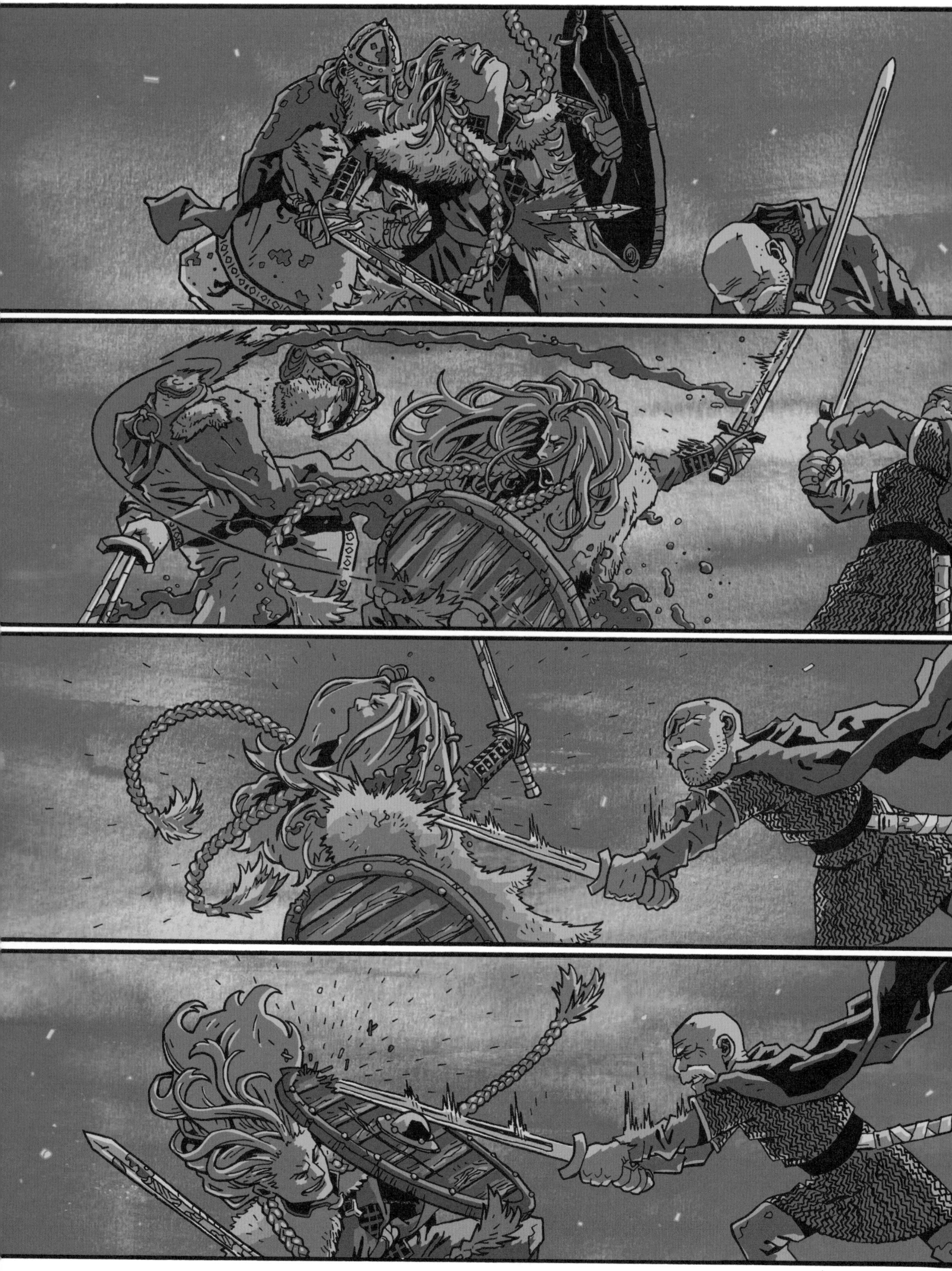

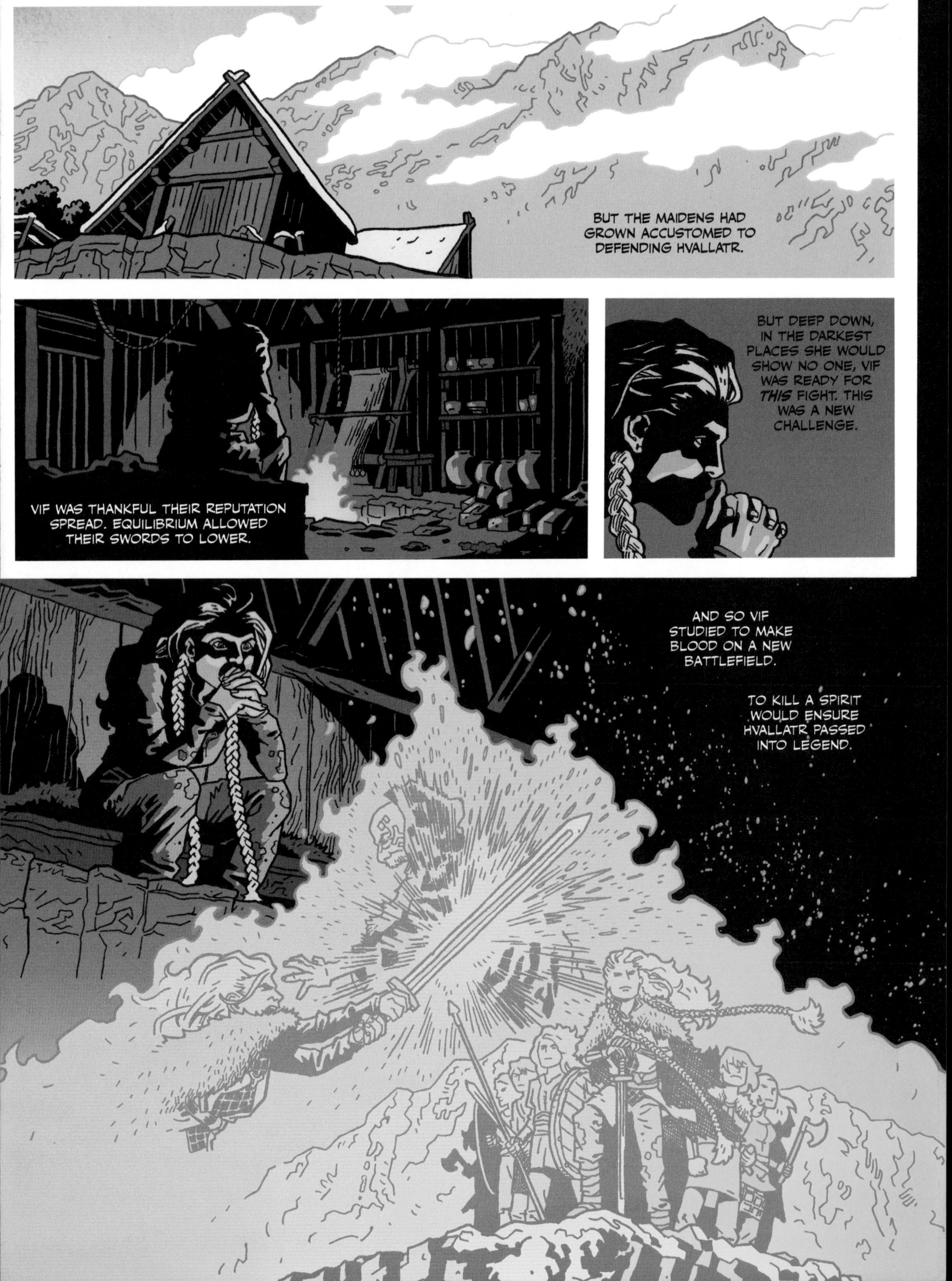
BUT THE MAIDENS HAD GROWN ACCUSTOMED TO DEFENDING HVALLATR.
VIF WAS THANKFUL THEIR REPUTATION SPREAD. EQUILIBRIUM ALLOWED THEIR SWORDS TO LOWER.
BUT DEEP DOWN, IN THE DARKEST PLACES SHE WOULD SHOW NO ONE, VIF WAS READY FOR *THIS* FIGHT. THIS WAS A NEW CHALLENGE.
AND SO VIF STUDIED TO MAKE BLOOD ON A NEW BATTLEFIELD.
TO KILL A SPIRIT WOULD ENSURE HVALLATR PASSED INTO LEGEND.

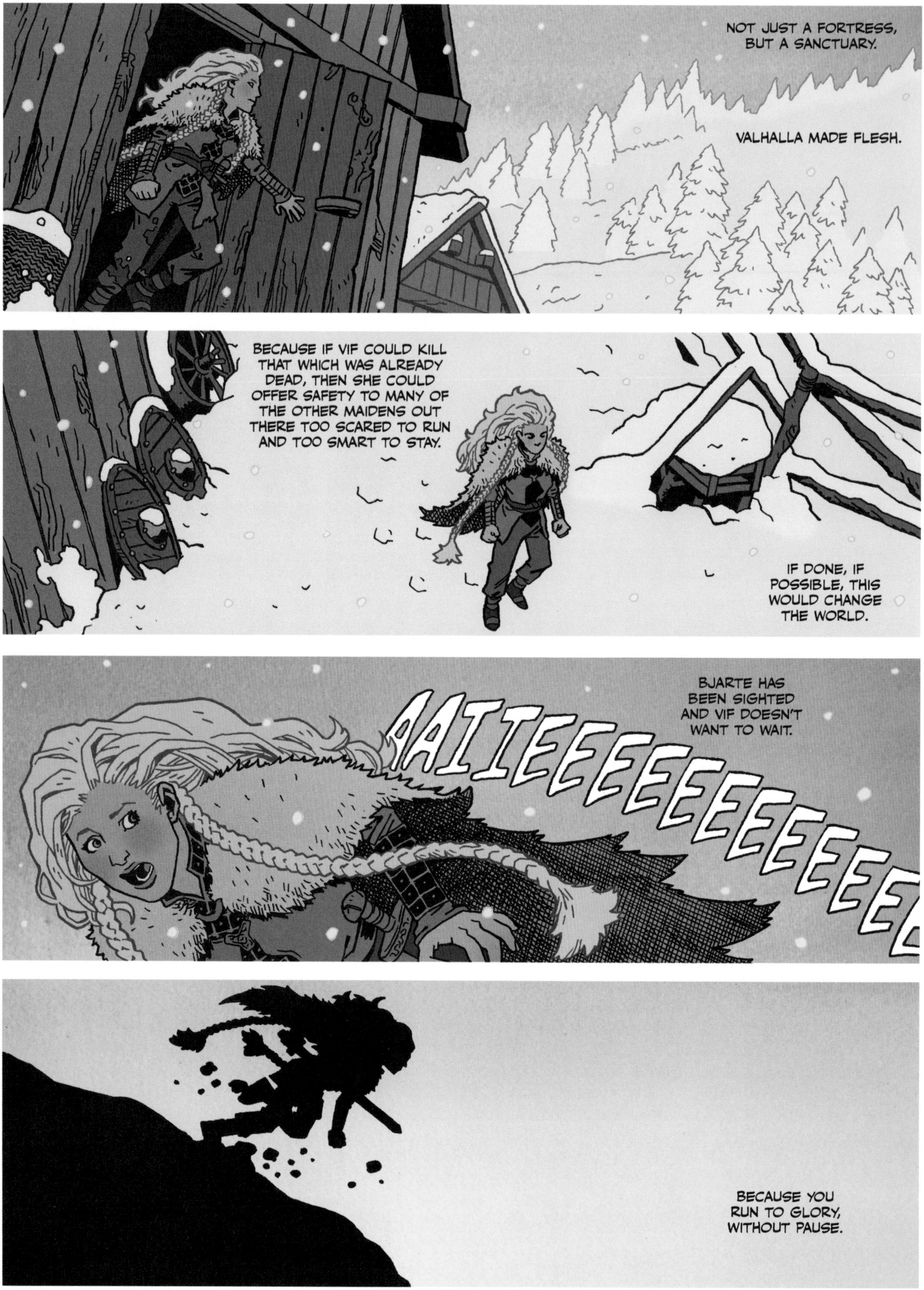
NOT JUST A FORTRESS, BUT A SANCTUARY.
VALHALLA MADE FLESH.
BECAUSE IF VIF COULD KILL THAT WHICH WAS ALREADY DEAD, THEN SHE COULD OFFER SAFETY TO MANY OF THE OTHER MAIDENS OUT THERE TOO SCARED TO RUN AND TOO SMART TO STAY.
IF DONE, IF POSSIBLE, THIS WOULD CHANGE THE WORLD.
BJARTE HAS BEEN SIGHTED AND VIF DOESN'T WANT TO WAIT.
AAIIEEEEEEEEEEEEEE
BECAUSE YOU RUN TO GLORY, WITHOUT PAUSE.

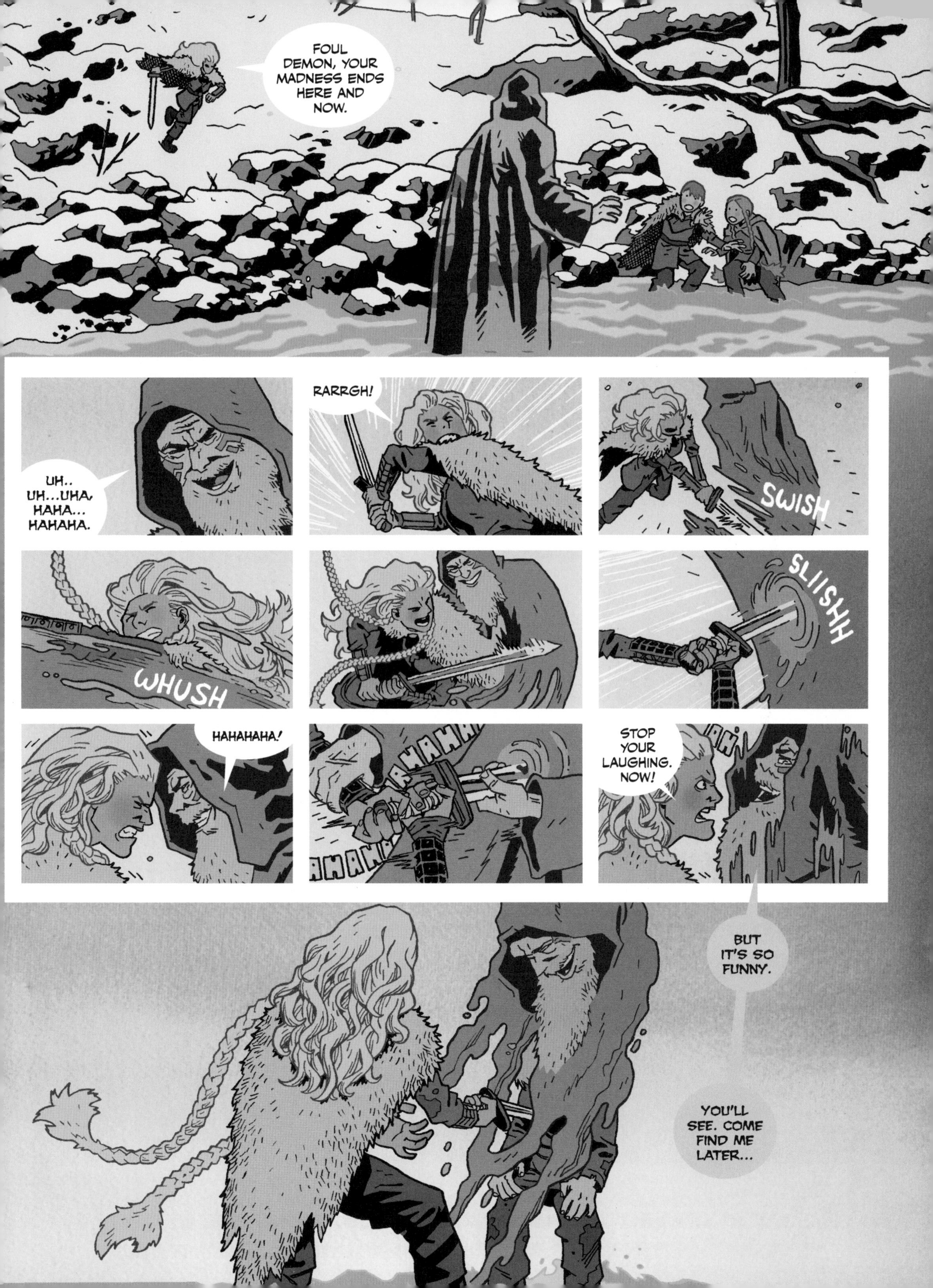
FOUL DEMON, YOUR MADNESS ENDS HERE AND NOW.
UH.. UH...UHA, HAHA... HAHAHA.
RARRGH!
SWISH
WHUSH
SLIISHH
HAHAHAHA!
STOP YOUR LAUGHING. NOW!
BUT IT'S SO FUNNY.
YOU'LL SEE. COME FIND ME LATER...

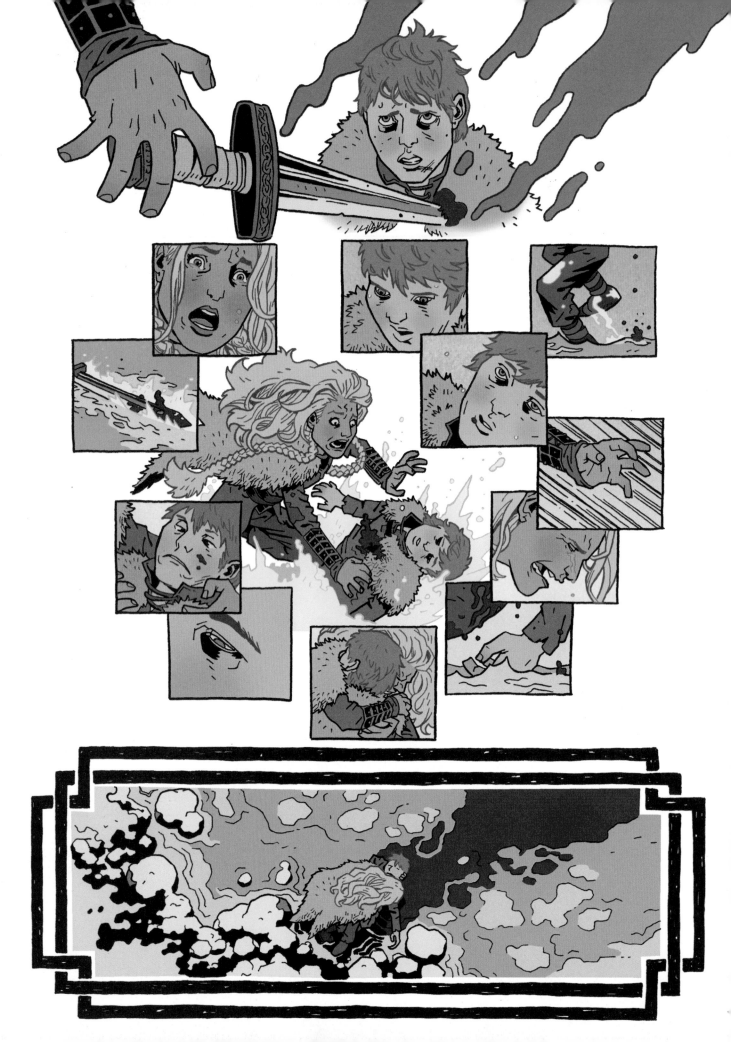

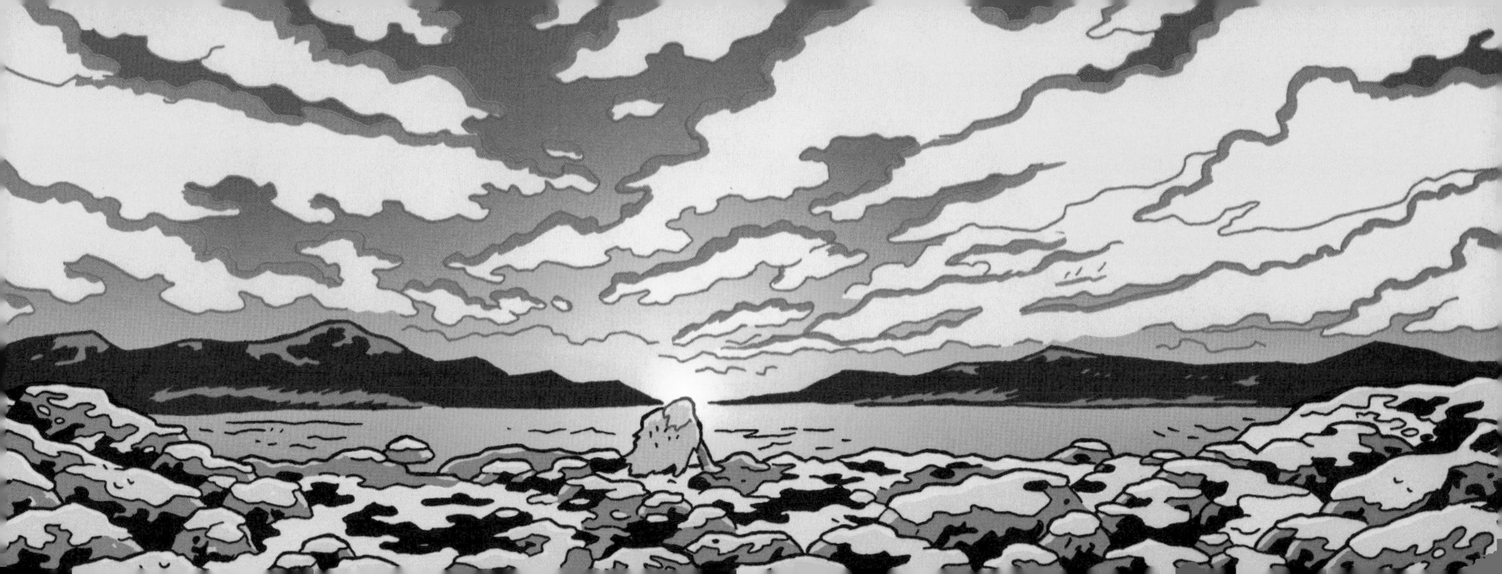

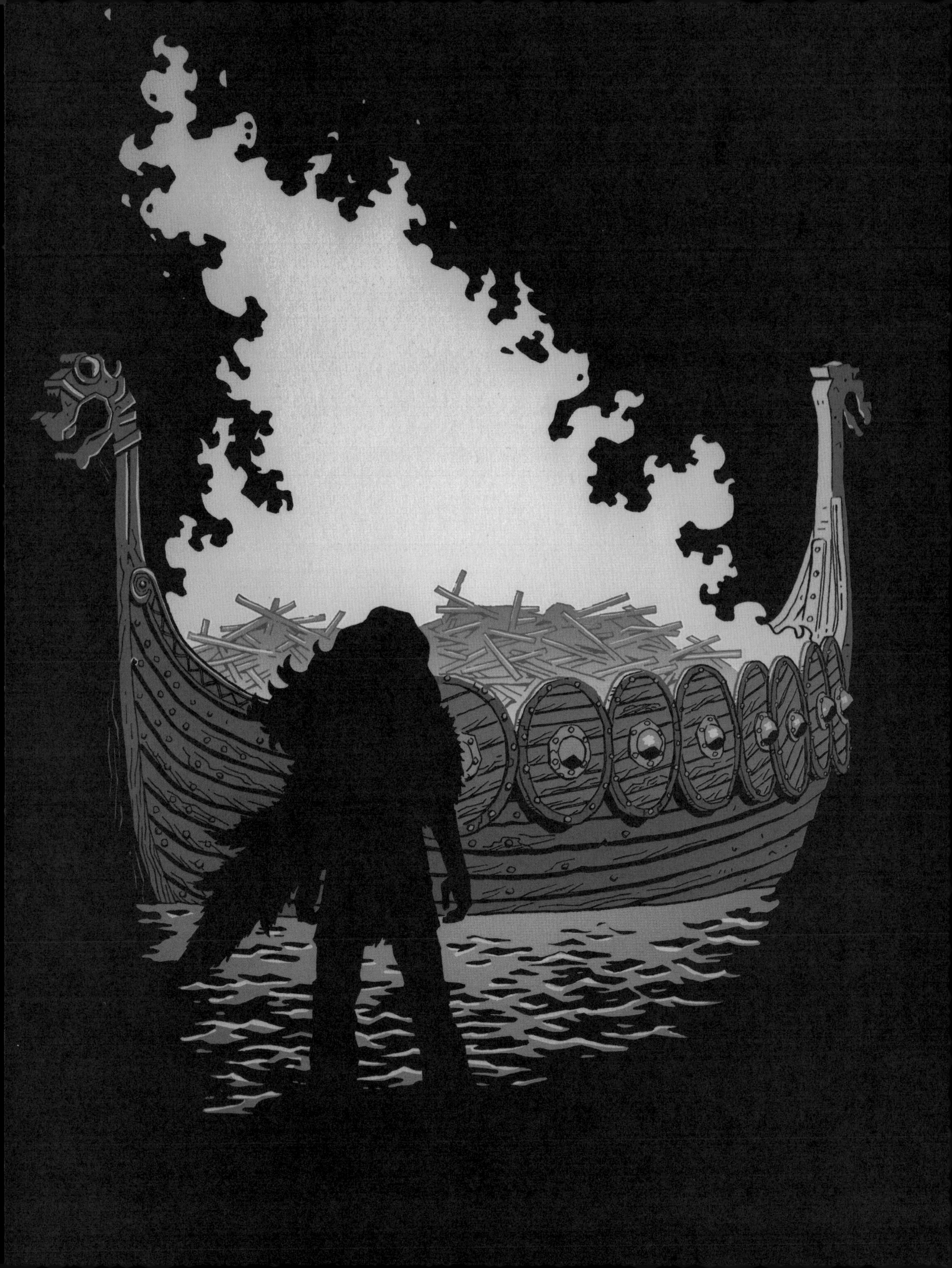

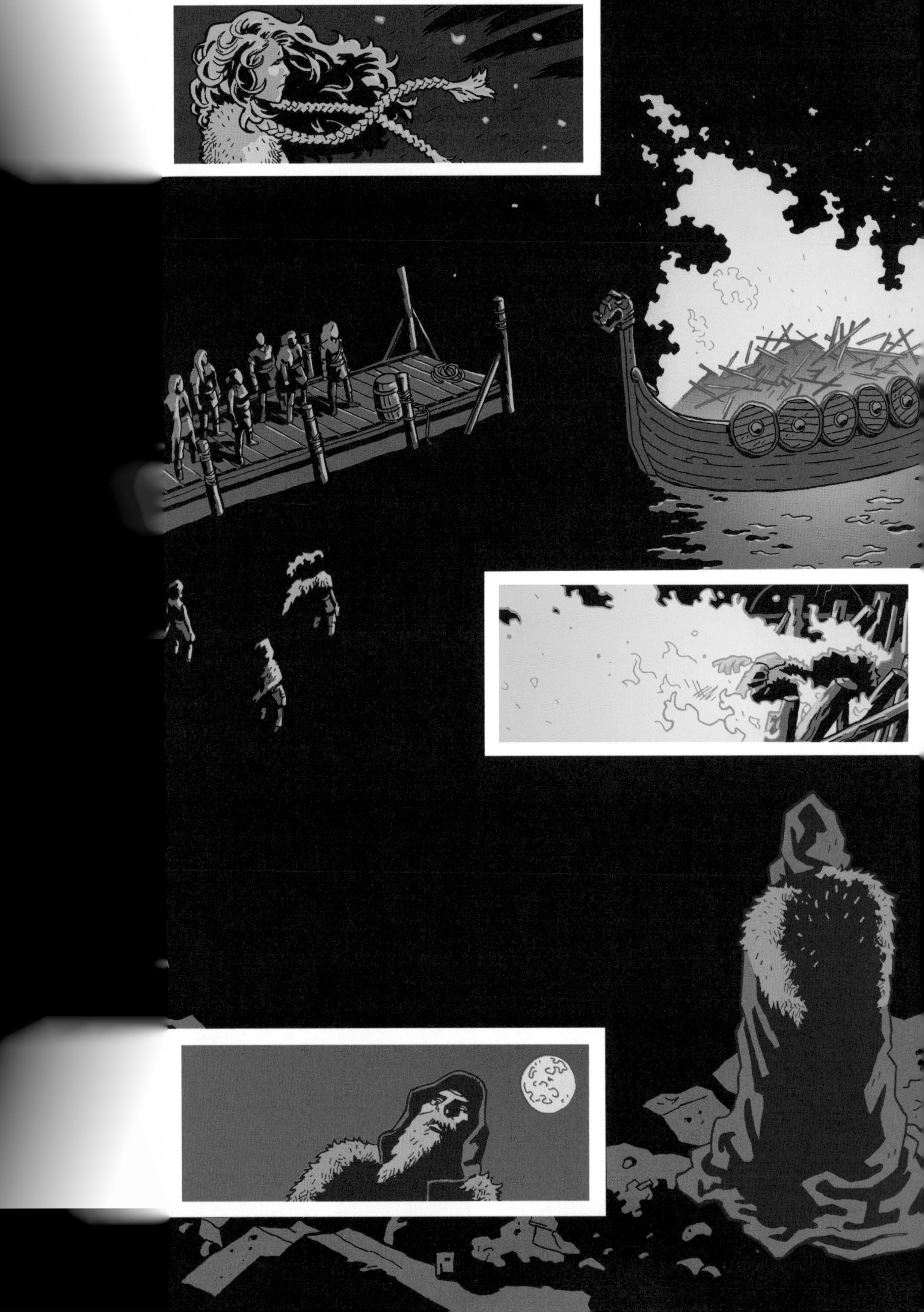

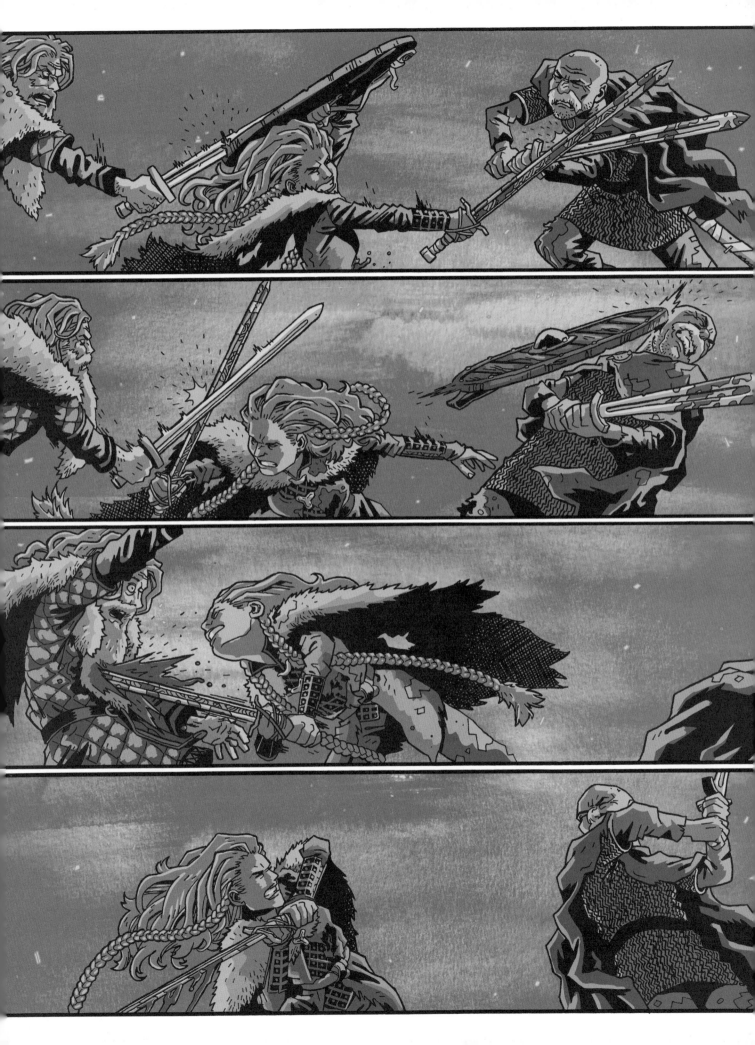

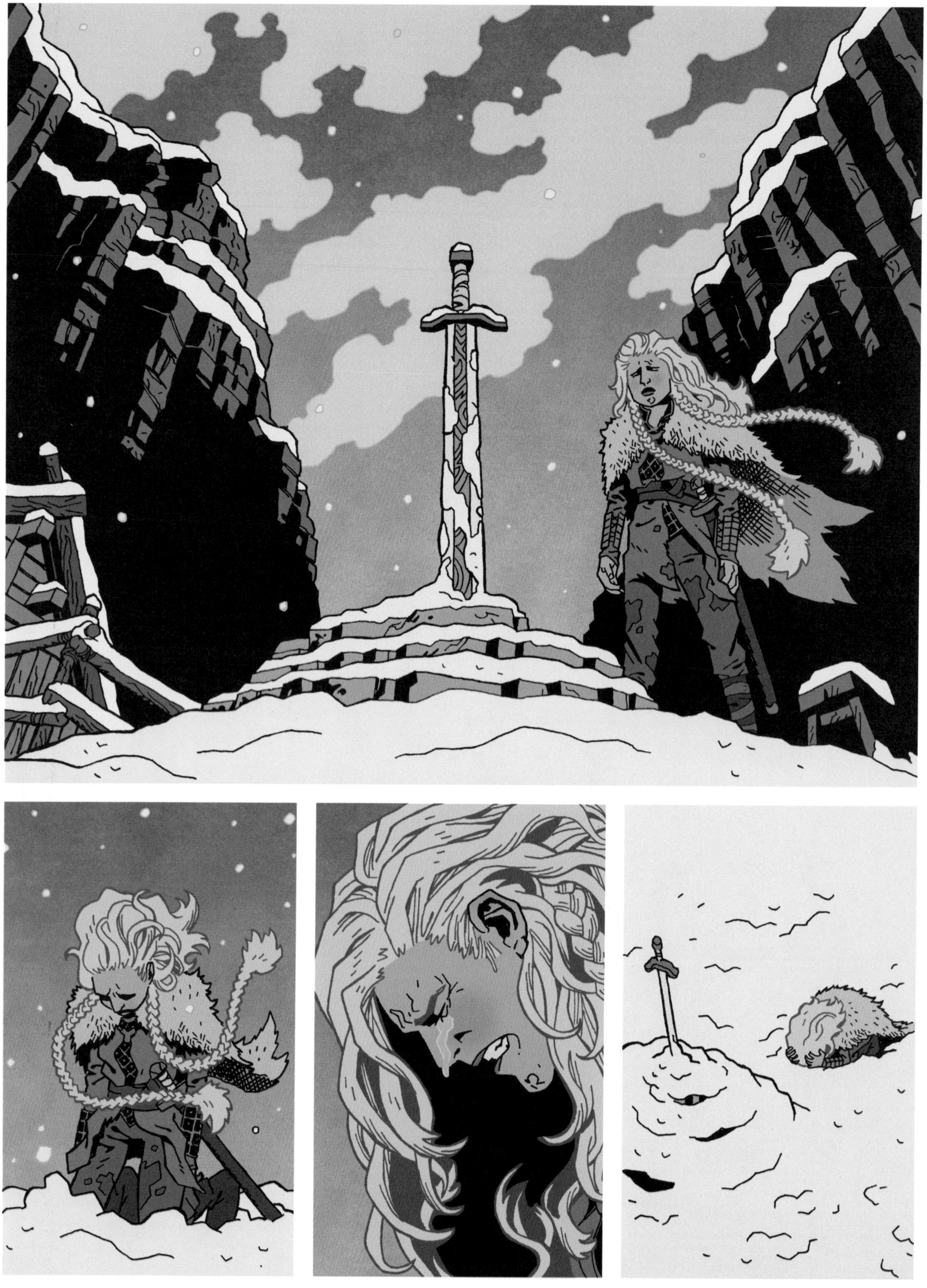

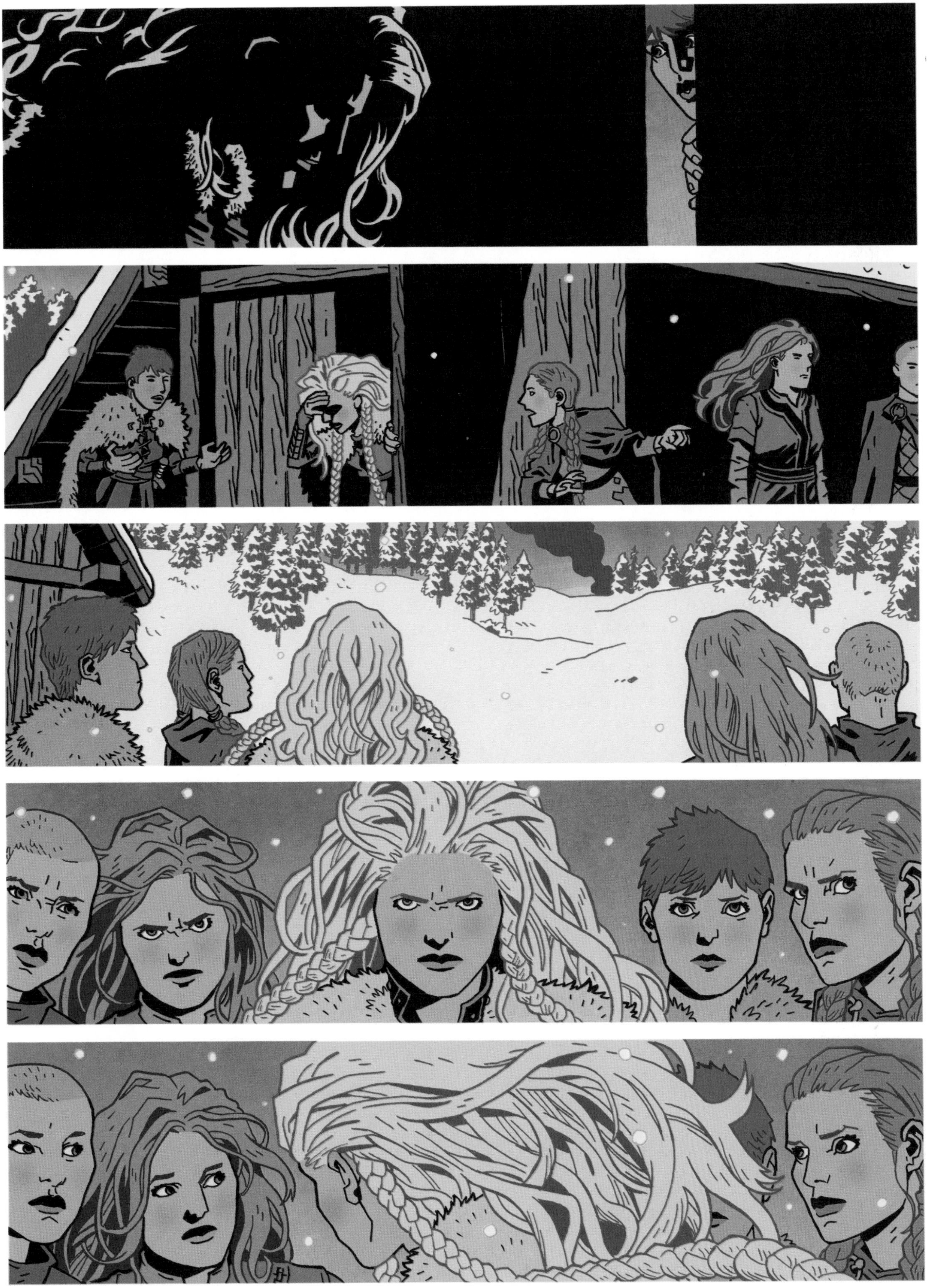

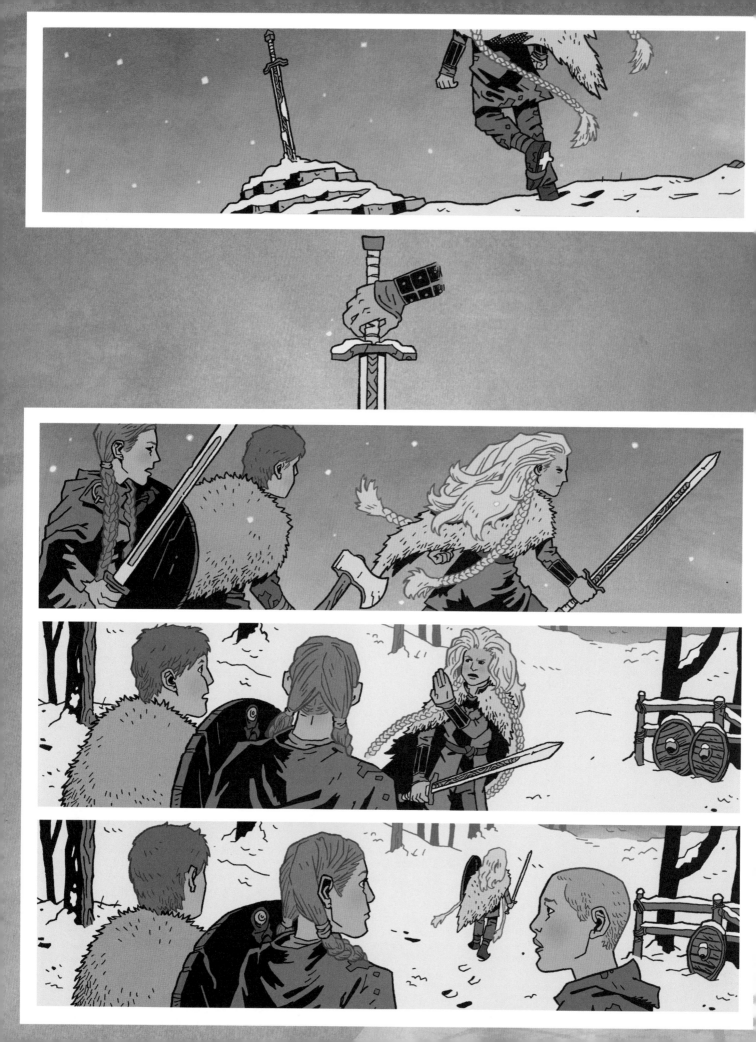

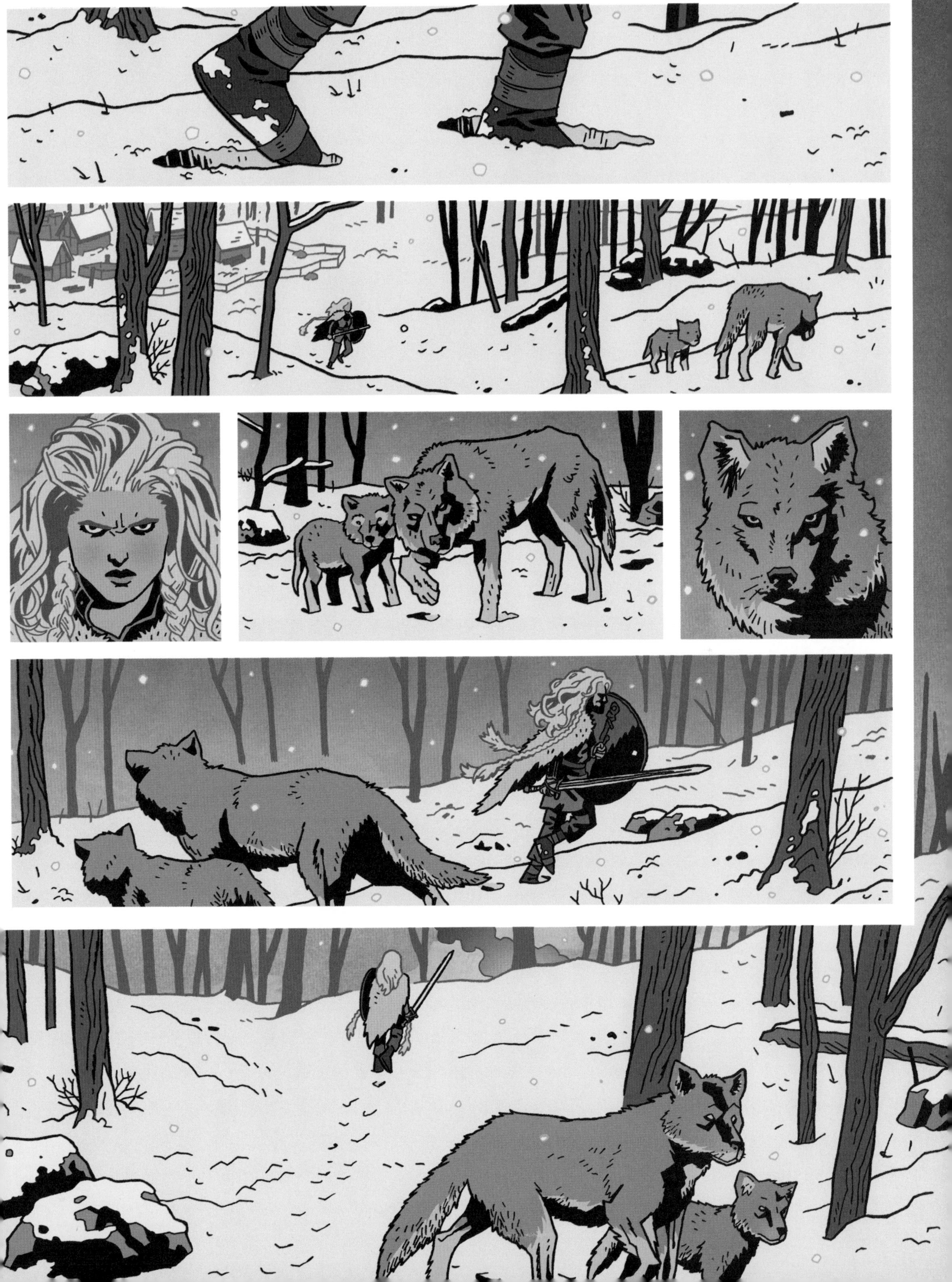

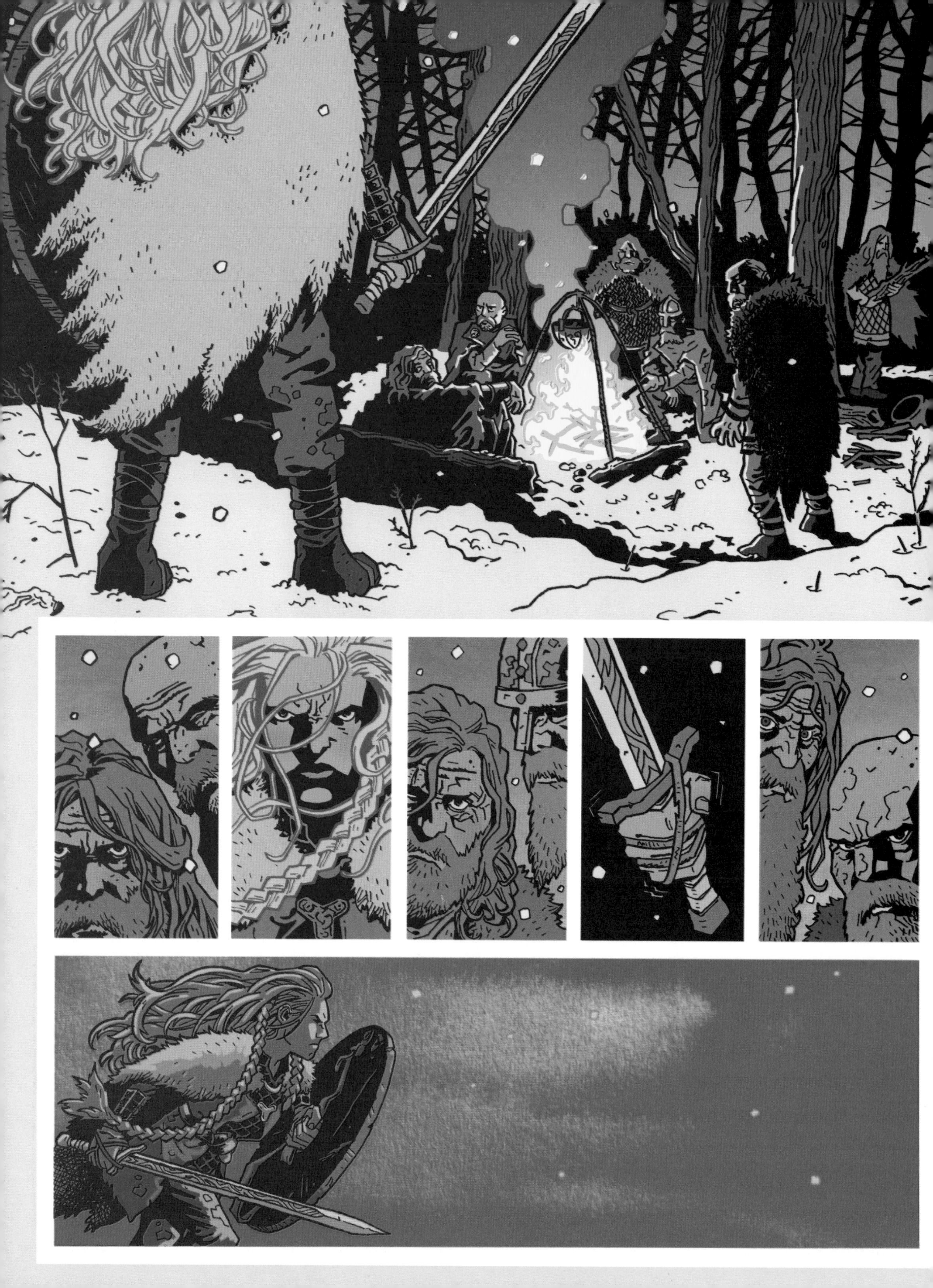

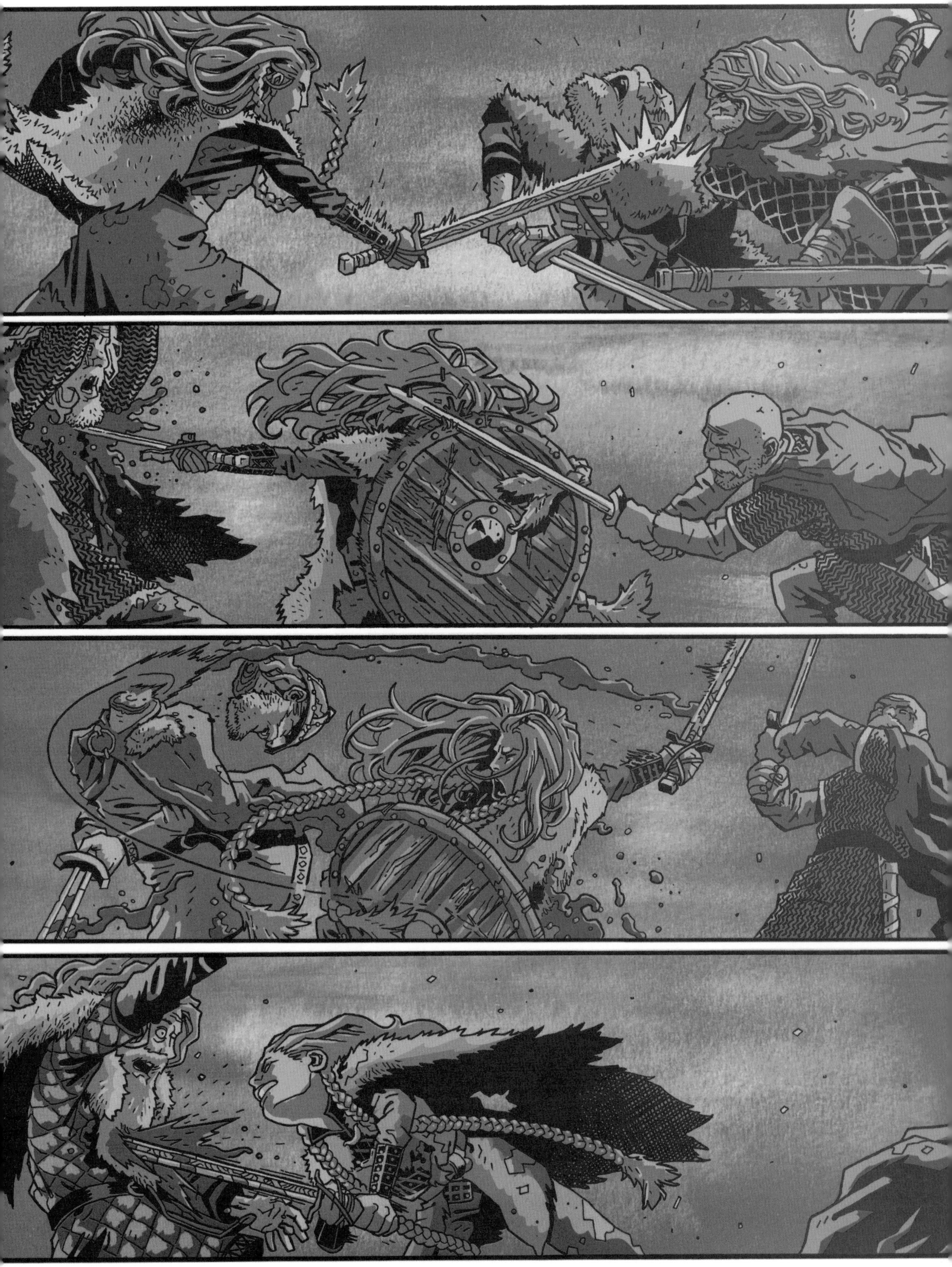

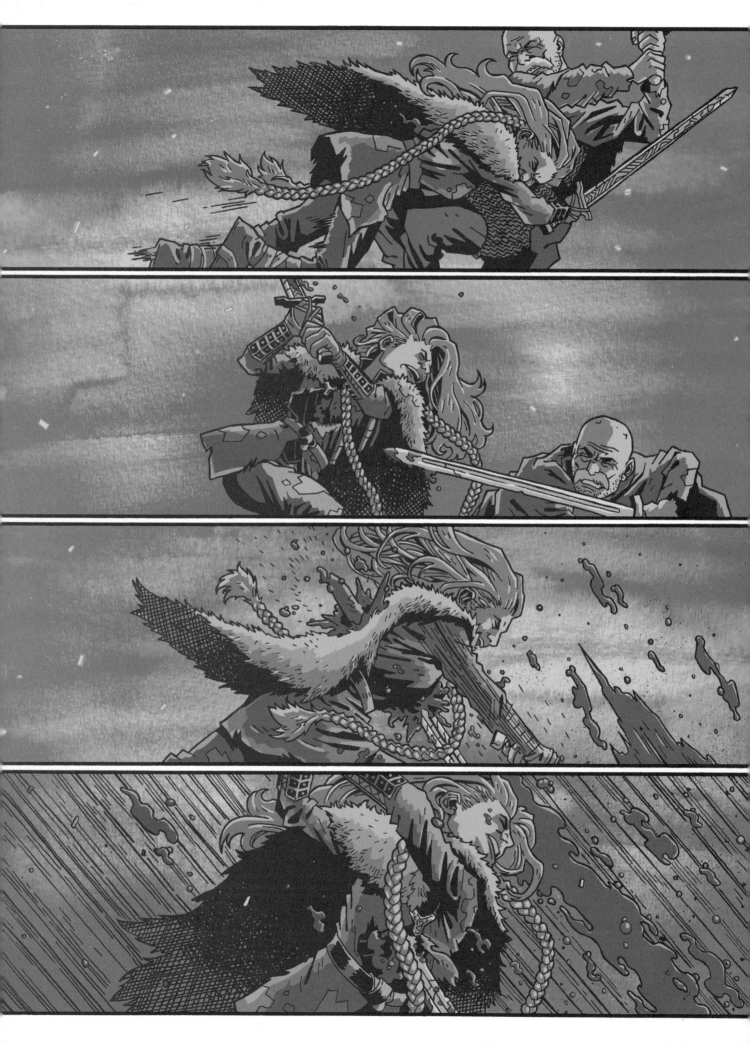

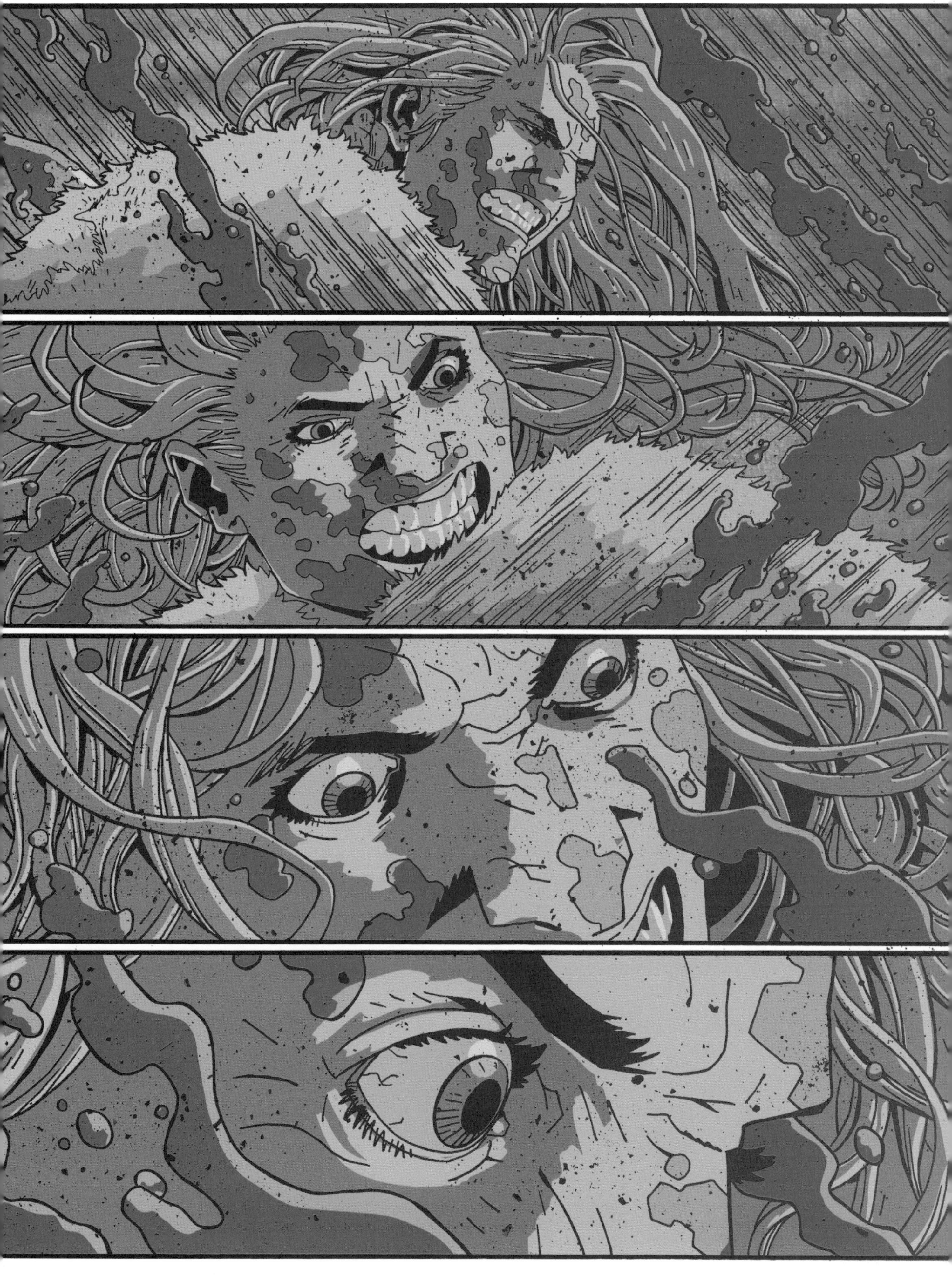

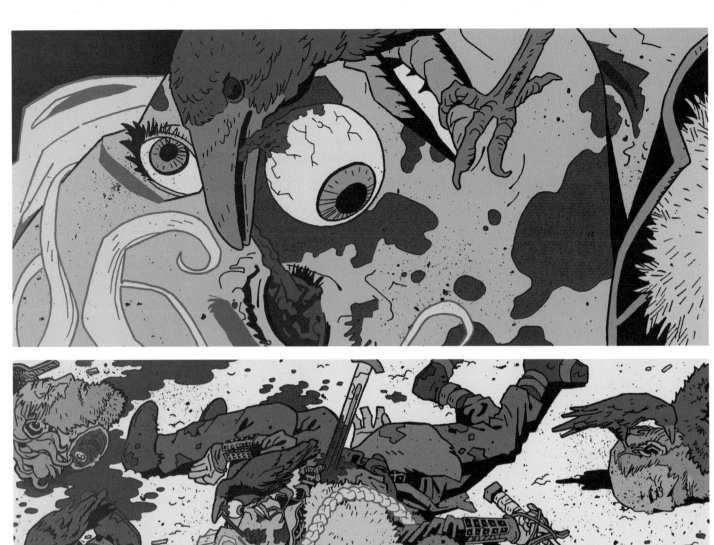

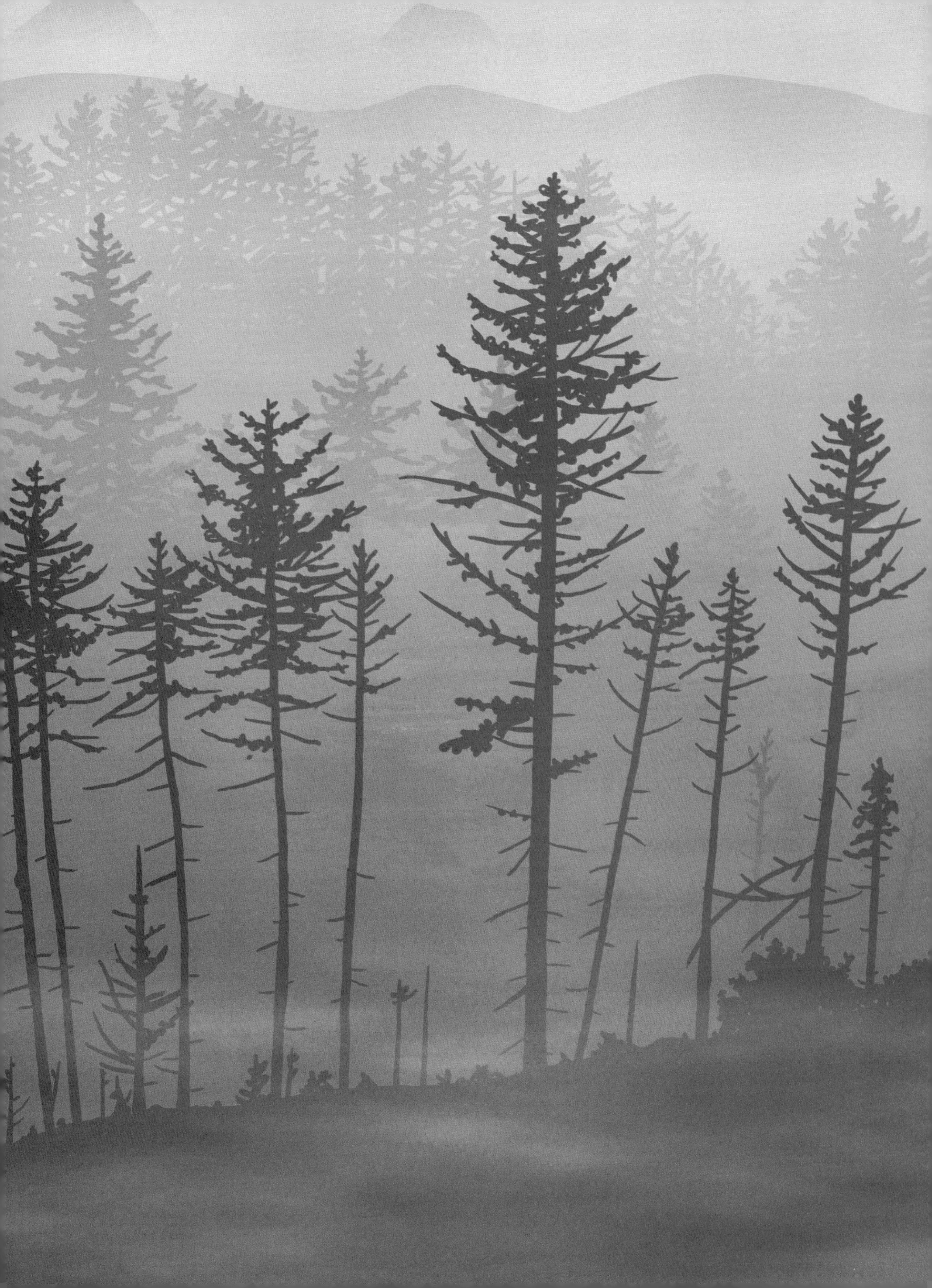

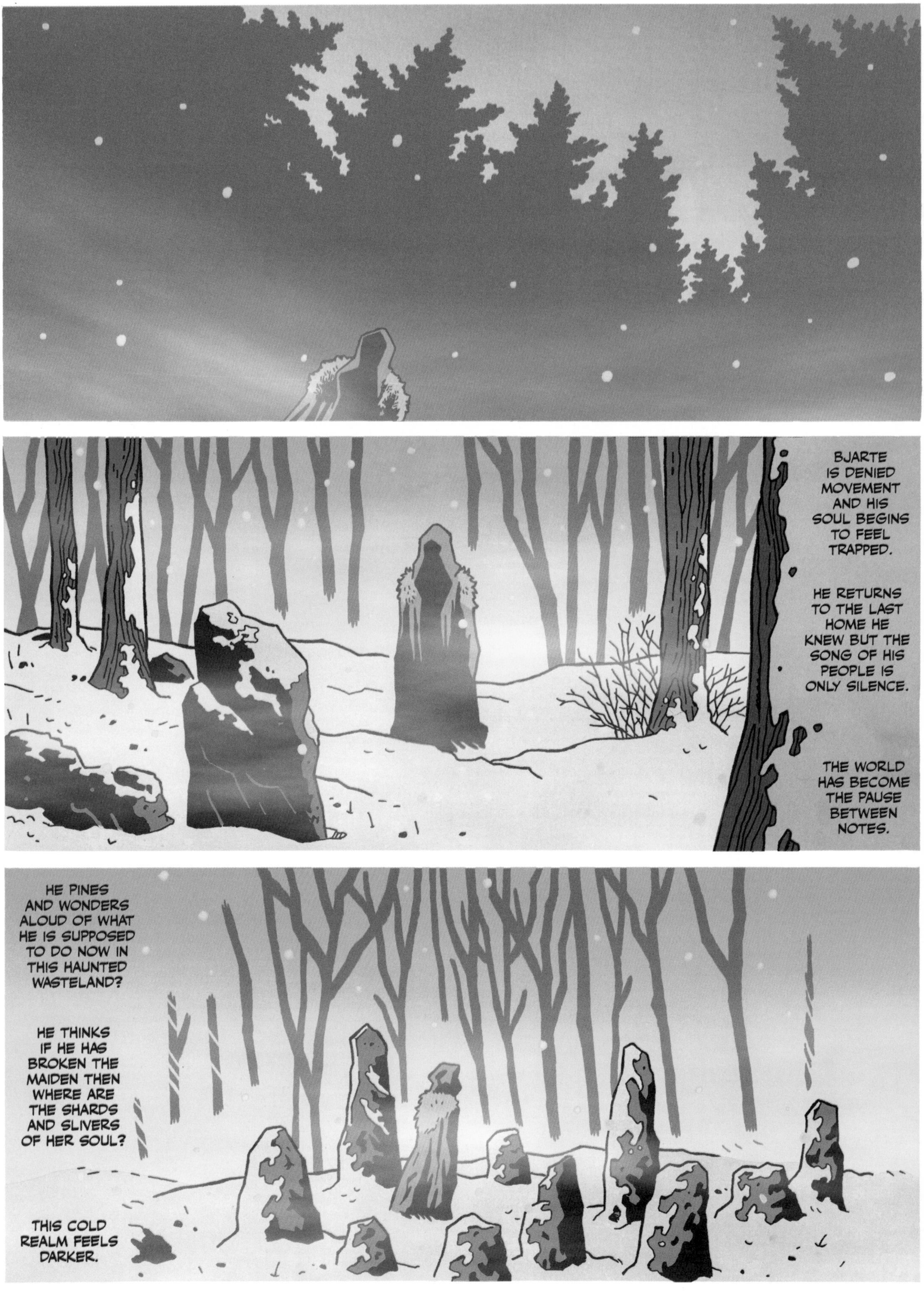
BJARTE IS DENIED MOVEMENT AND HIS SOUL BEGINS TO FEEL TRAPPED.
HE RETURNS TO THE LAST HOME HE KNEW BUT THE SONG OF HIS PEOPLE IS ONLY SILENCE.
THE WORLD HAS BECOME THE PAUSE BETWEEN NOTES.
HE PINES AND WONDERS ALOUD OF WHAT HE IS SUPPOSED TO DO NOW IN THIS HAUNTED WASTELAND?
HE THINKS IF HE HAS BROKEN THE MAIDEN THEN WHERE ARE THE SHARDS AND SLIVERS OF HER SOUL?
THIS COLD REALM FEELS DARKER.

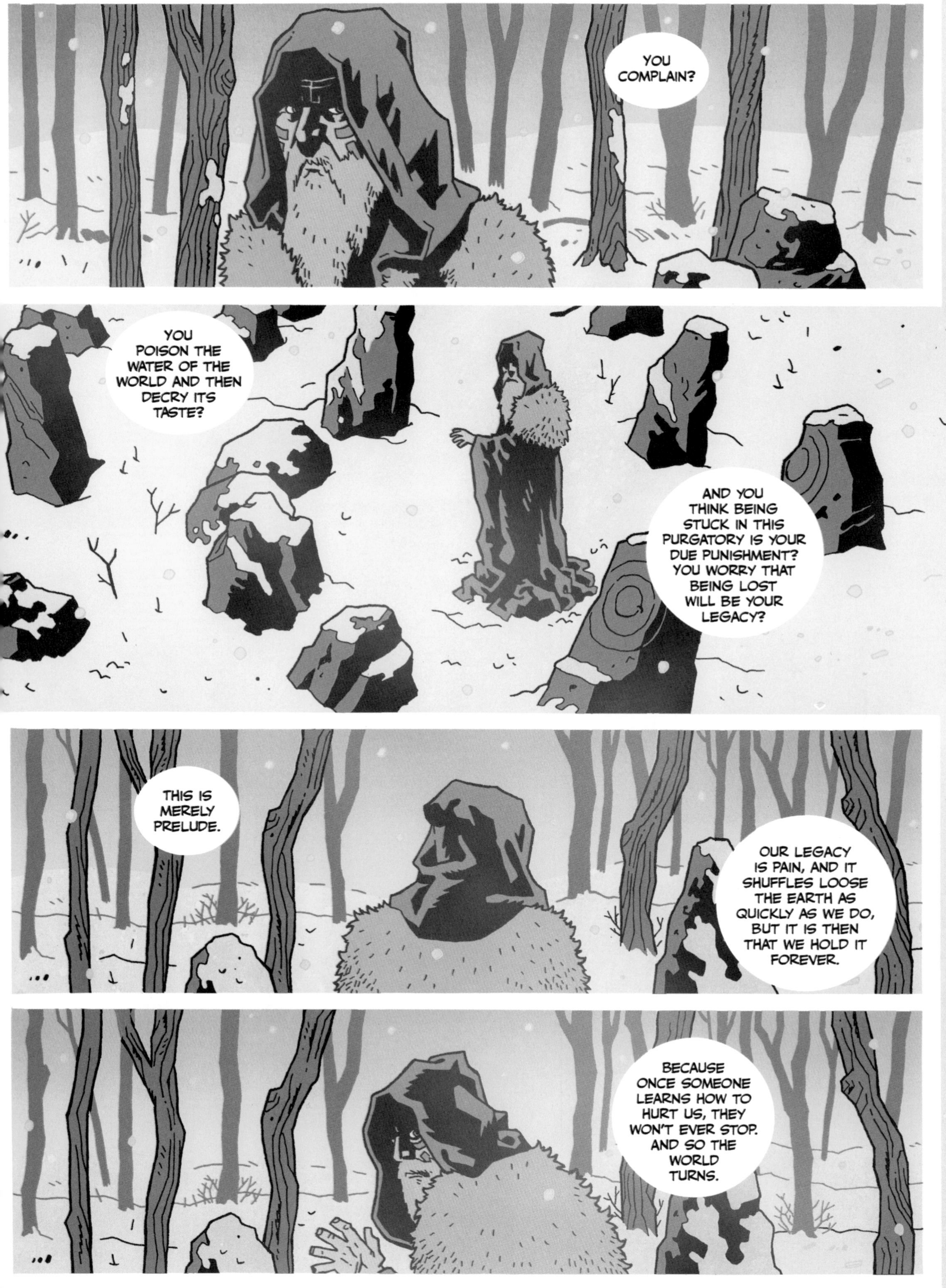
YOU COMPLAIN?
YOU POISON THE WATER OF THE WORLD AND THEN DECRY ITS TASTE?
AND YOU THINK BEING STUCK IN THIS PURGATORY IS YOUR DUE PUNISHMENT? YOU WORRY THAT BEING LOST WILL BE YOUR LEGACY?
THIS IS MERELY PRELUDE.
OUR LEGACY IS PAIN, AND IT SHUFFLES LOOSE THE EARTH AS QUICKLY AS WE DO, BUT IT IS THEN THAT WE HOLD IT FOREVER.
BECAUSE ONCE SOMEONE LEARNS HOW TO HURT US, THEY WON'T EVER STOP. AND SO THE WORLD TURNS.

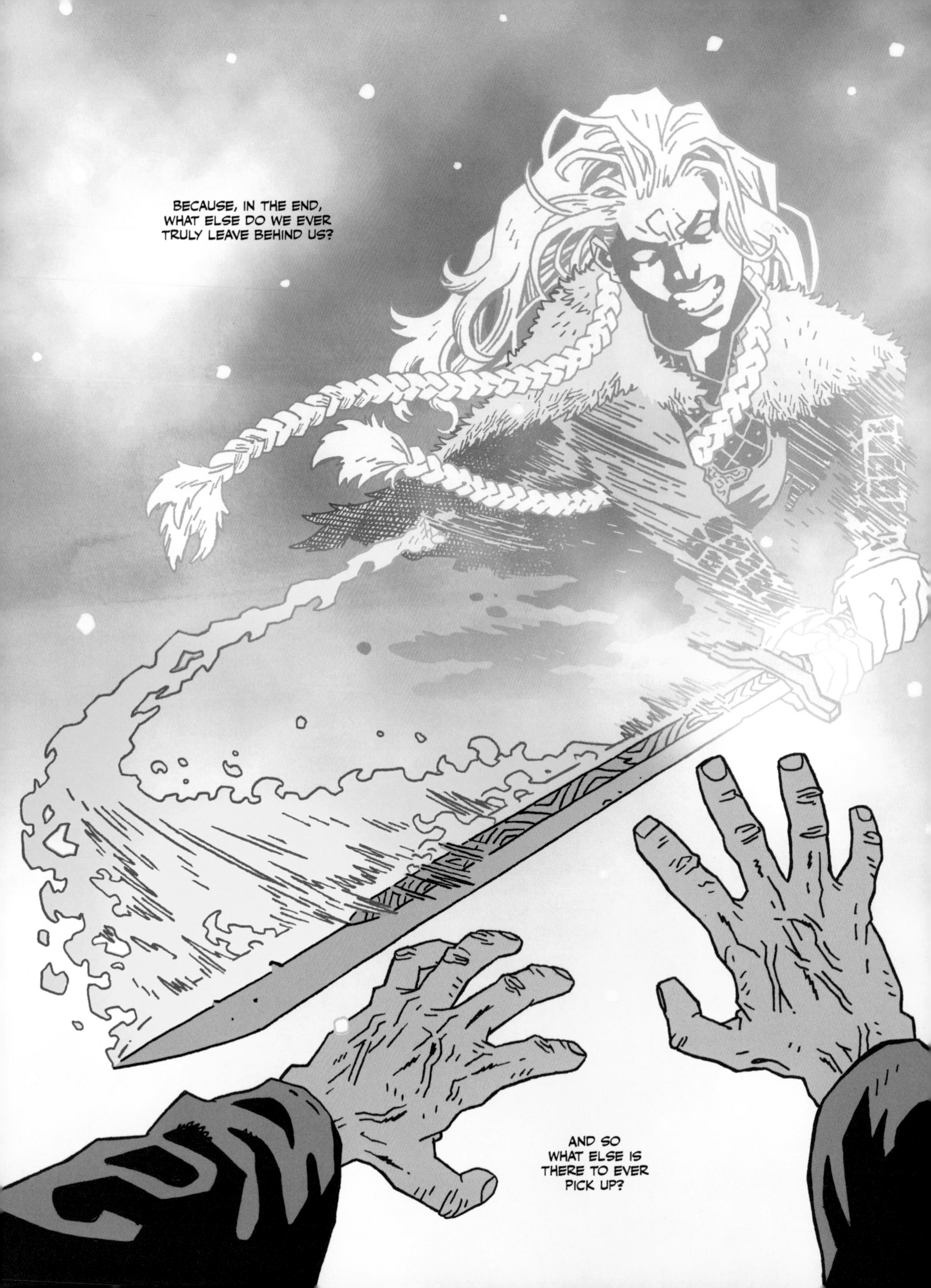
BECAUSE, IN THE END, WHAT ELSE DO WE EVER TRULY LEAVE BEHIND US?
AND SO WHAT ELSE IS THERE TO EVER PICK UP?

Truth, Beauty, Erudition - Pick Two

I wrote this comic for Eric Zawadzki.

I would have shelved this script if Eric couldn't do it. Which is why it took us ~3 years to get this baby onto shelves. Eric had to go off and illustrate THE DREGS - go now, buy, read, reread, you're welcome - and when he did give time to this collaboration he made certain he did not go easy on himself.

Y'see, I sent Eric a script for 24 pages. But he dug it so much that he wanted to really explore the themes of the book visually. He wanted to draw things out, make things matter, and not be beholden to arbitrary issue numbers. And I swear every time he sat down to this beast he added more pages for himself.

So here we are. This story ran over, twice as long, and is easily triple the quality in which it started in my head. The fights became more intricate and brutal, the horizon simply wouldn't end, and the emotions started to tunnel down so deep they broke through the mantle and now everything's coming up from way down there.

This is what beautiful collaboration feels like.

There are dream genres into which I want to eventually g[r]ift great stories. I'll eventually crack the werewolf story dna, and I'm certain the perfect heist plan will one day lay out in my head. But for now I am settling into the happiness of knowing I'll never be a part of a better Viking tale than what we have here with our shieldmaidens. Everything here is special to us and we hope it connects with readers willing to sit down and slowly let every page sink into their hearts.

At the centre of every story I create, I want there to be human truth. And at the end of every story I create, I want you to be pushed to go find what you feel next on your own.

Doing this with scumbag mystical ghosts and hyperintense fight scenes just makes it all the more beautiful.

Doing it with my mates Eric and Dee and Dan and Matt makes it perfection.

Thank you for coming viking with us.

Ryan K Lindsay
October, 2017.
Still looking over Eric's art and trying to understand the arcane alchemy at work.

CONCEPT ART

After finishing our previous comics collaboration, *Headspace*, Ryan sent me his short script for *Eternal* and I immediately fell in love with it. Although I was too busy with other projects, I managed to find some time to do some quick concept art. I wanted to get a feel for the overall look of the story.

In the time since drawing these, we had various discussions and the story went through several changes.

Eric Zawadzki

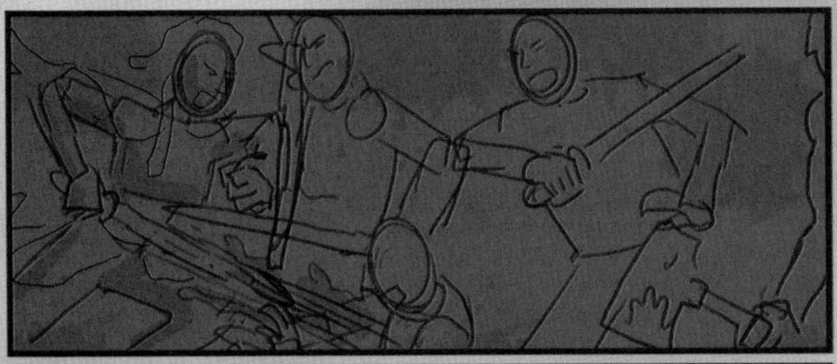

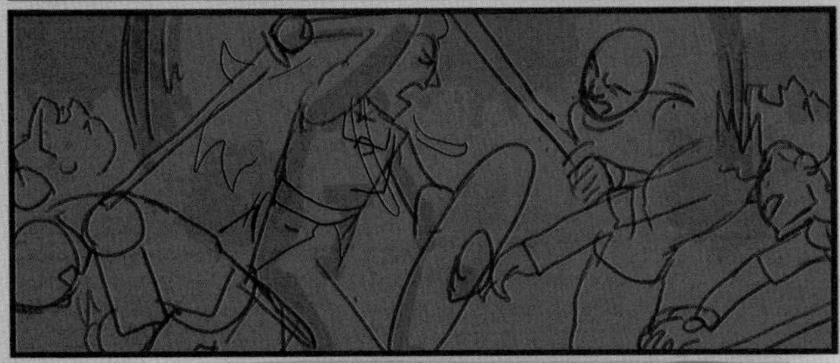

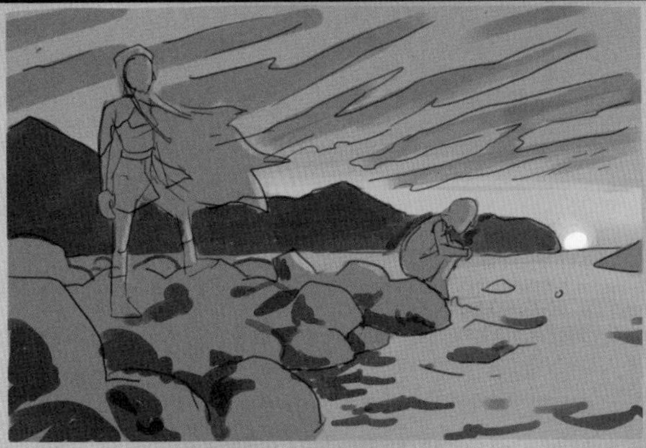

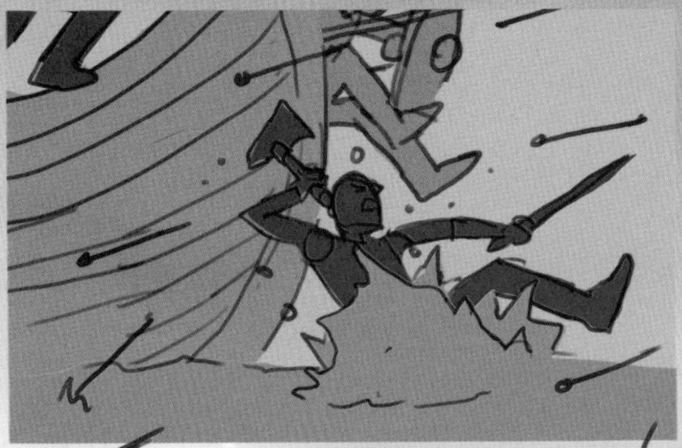

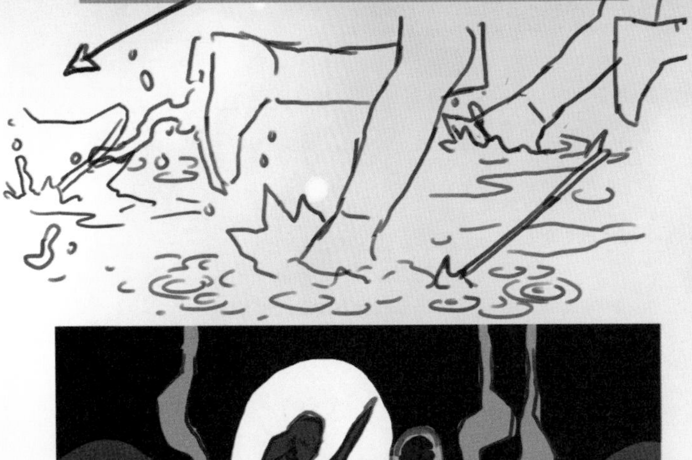

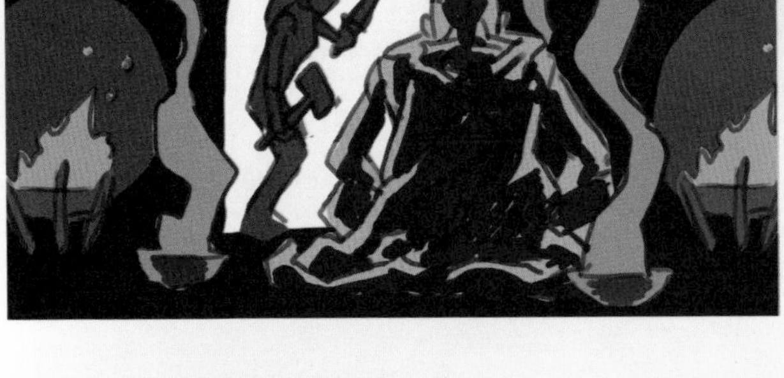

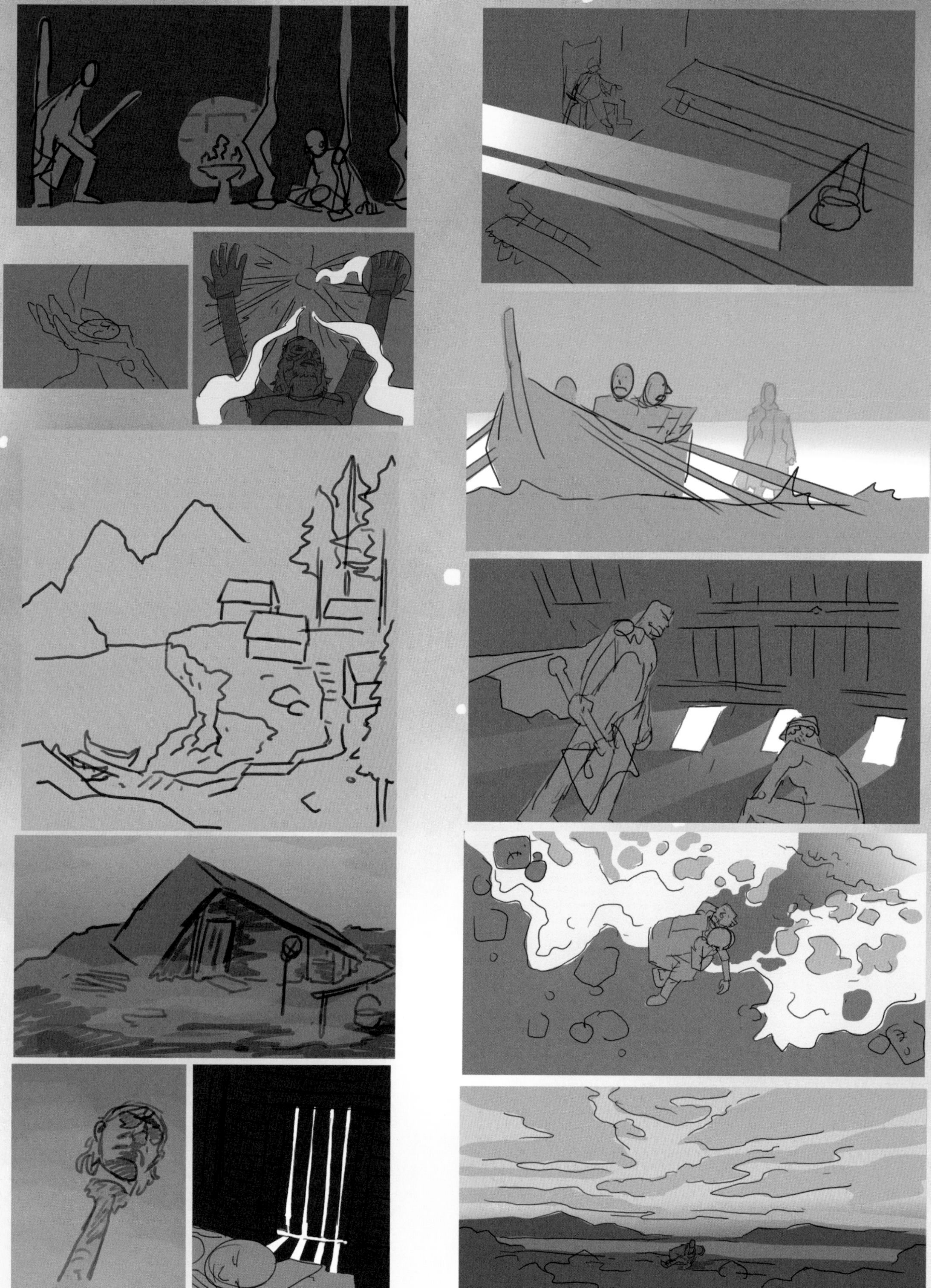

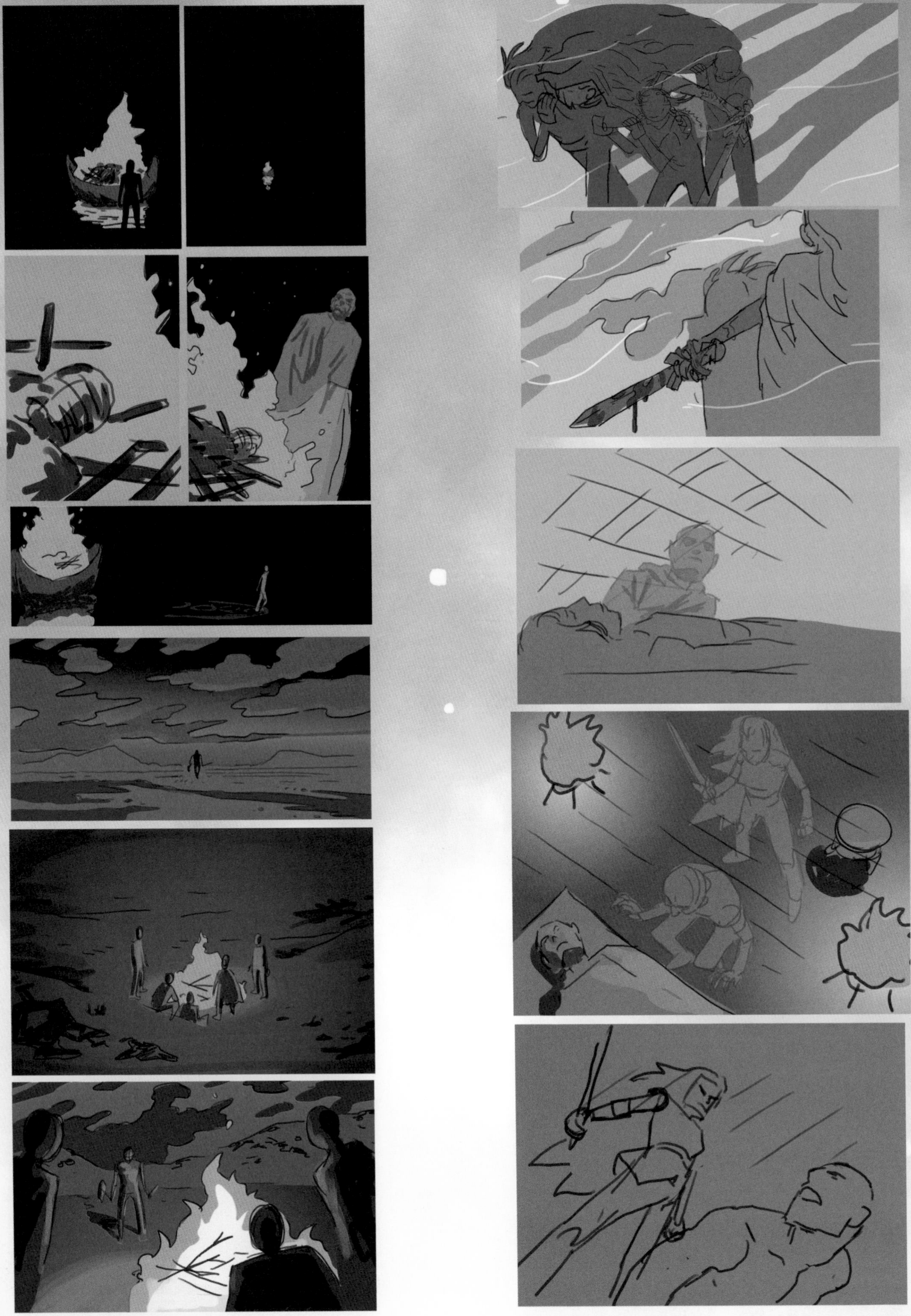

I decided to do a test page several years ago, in between other gigs. These are the various ideas I went through. The final version I arrived at with this test page differs significantly from what was eventually published, though. When it came down to finally drawing the project, another idea came to me.

Eric Zawadzki

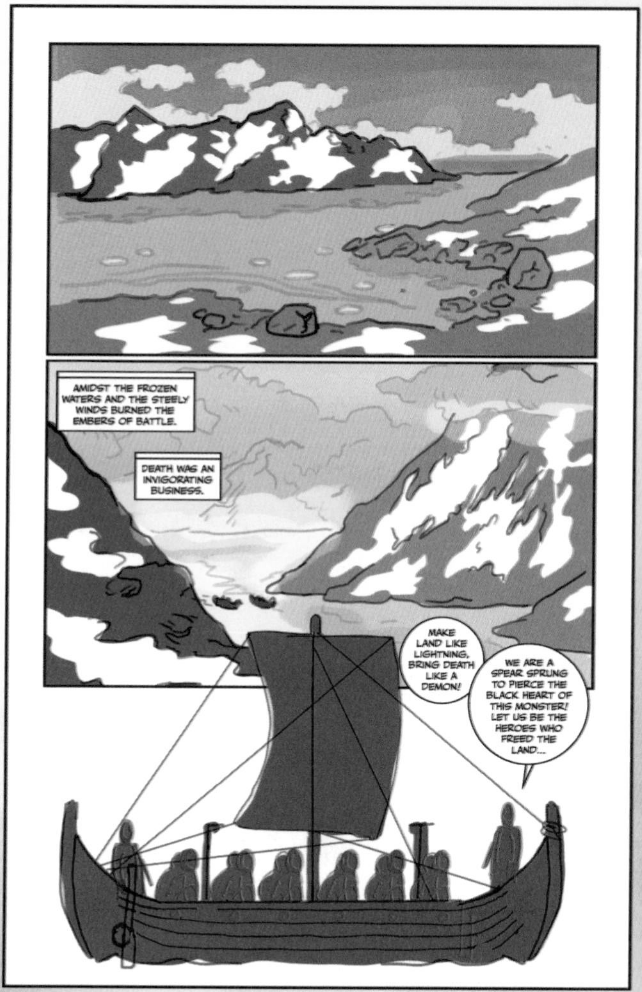
AMIDST THE FROZEN WATERS AND THE STEELY WINDS BURNED THE EMBERS OF BATTLE.
DEATH WAS AN INVIGORATING BUSINESS.
MAKE LAND LIKE LIGHTNING, BRING DEATH LIKE A DEMON!
WE ARE A SPEAR SPRUNG TO PIERCE THE BLACK HEART OF THIS MONSTER! LET US BE THE HEROES WHO FREED THE LAND...

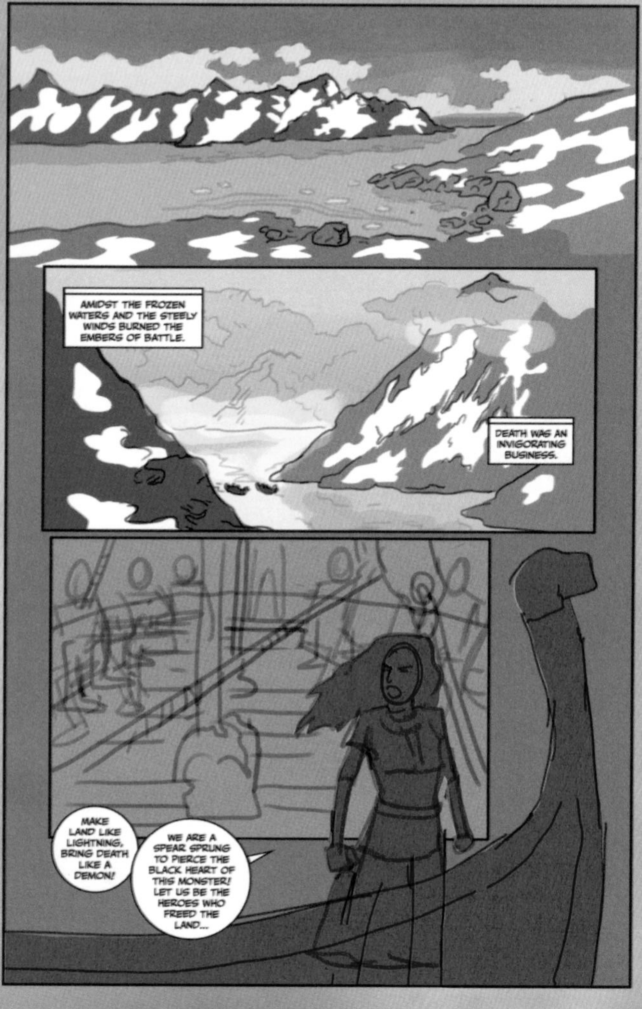
AMIDST THE FROZEN WATERS AND THE STEELY WINDS BURNED THE EMBERS OF BATTLE.
DEATH WAS AN INVIGORATING BUSINESS.
MAKE LAND LIKE LIGHTNING, BRING DEATH LIKE A DEMON!
WE ARE A SPEAR SPRUNG TO PIERCE THE BLACK HEART OF THIS MONSTER! LET US BE THE HEROES WHO FREED THE LAND...

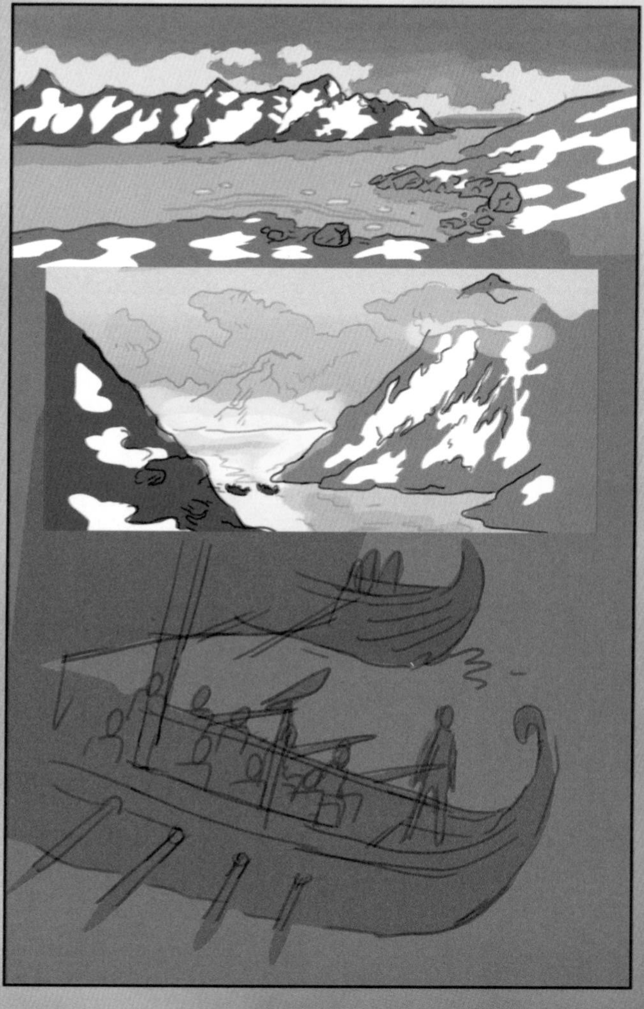

This was the final version of that test page. I assumed we wouldn't be able to bring on a colorist, so I decided to test out a more basic look, so that I could save some time. Thankfully, we got Dee on board. He's also much better than I am with color.

Eric Zawadzki

These are the rough layouts for the finale. We were originally going to reveal Vif's ghost form earlier, but that would have undercut the drama of the final page.

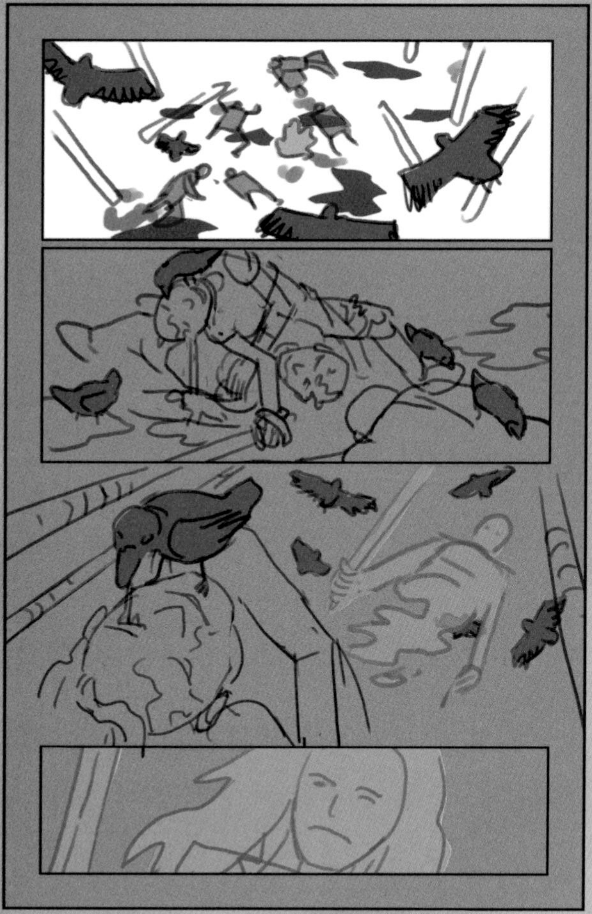

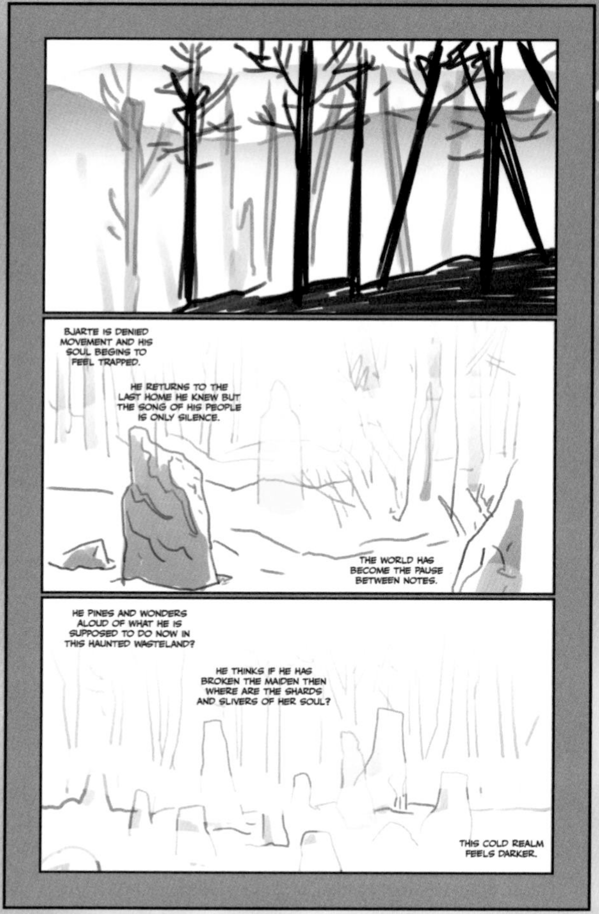
BJARTE IS DENIED MOVEMENT AND HIS SOUL BEGINS TO FEEL TRAPPED.
HE RETURNS TO THE LAST HOME HE KNEW BUT THE SONG OF HIS PEOPLE IS ONLY SILENCE.
THE WORLD HAS BECOME THE PAUSE BETWEEN NOTES.
HE PINES AND WONDERS ALOUD OF WHAT HE IS SUPPOSED TO DO NOW IN THIS HAUNTED WASTELAND?
HE THINKS IF HE HAS BROKEN THE MAIDEN THEN WHERE ARE THE SHARDS AND SLIVERS OF HER SOUL?
THIS COLD REALM FEELS DARKER.

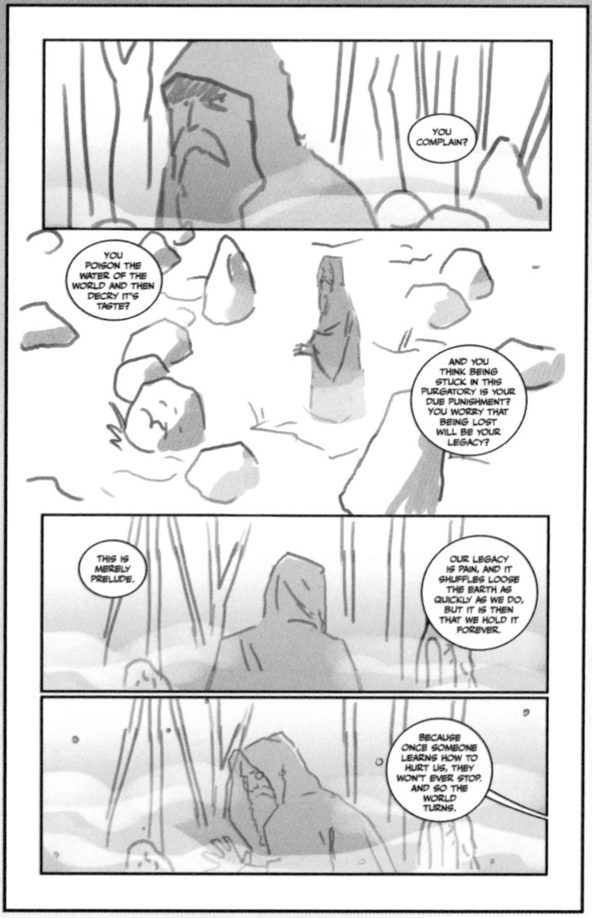
YOU COMPLAIN?
YOU POISON THE WATER OF THE WORLD AND THEN DECRY IT'S TASTE?
AND YOU THINK BEING STUCK IN THIS PURGATORY IS YOUR DUE PUNISHMENT? YOU WORRY THAT BEING LOST WILL BE YOUR LEGACY?
THIS IS MERELY PRELUDE.
OUR LEGACY IS PAIN, AND IT SHUFFLES LOOSE THE EARTH AS QUICKLY AS WE DO, BUT IT IS THEN THAT WE HOLD IT FOREVER.
BECAUSE ONCE SOMEONE LEARNS HOW TO HURT US, THEY WON'T EVER STOP, AND SO THE WORLD TURNS.

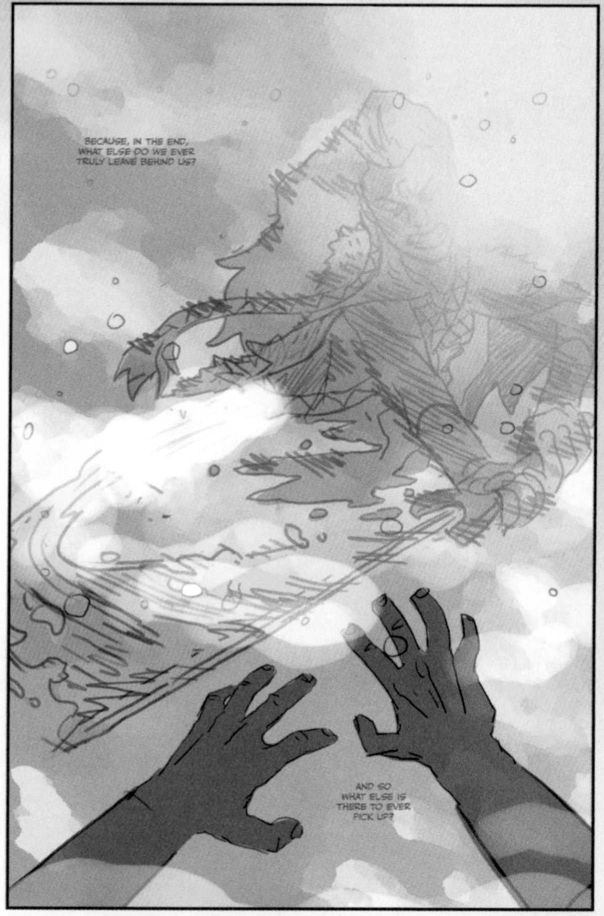
BECAUSE, IN THE END, WHAT ELSE DO WE EVER TRULY LEAVE BEHIND US?
AND SO WHAT ELSE IS THERE TO EVER PICK UP?

Eternal cover inks by

eric zawadzki

craft corner

by dee cunniffe

This piece originally ran in *PanelxPanel* #7, a magazine about comics appreciation and analysis created by Hassan Otsmane-Elhaou.

Sitting down to a new project is always a daunting and exciting moment. It's an opportunity to try out some new techniques and styles.

When that initial email comes in offering you the chance to jump in to a new world there's always a few questions I ask: who is the artist? What's the deadline and what's the page rate? The first two are very important, the third not so much. The artist I'll be coloring is a big priority for me, because I really feel that I need to be able to mesh well with their art. If my coloring style doesn't match then I can totally ruin the project and, personally, it can feel very disheartening to slog through a book I'm not enjoying working on!

The deadline and schedule are important too, I don't want to double-book myself for a week or two, I try not to do all nighters, and I do like to spend time with my kids! The page rate is not necessarily too important, while I do like to pay my bills and put food on the table, I will work on a project that doesn't pay great but has a great story to tell or a fantastic creative team I want to work with.

I address this because I got an email about working on a new book not too long ago. It's what became *Eternal,* with Ryan K Lindsay and Eric Zawadzki.

Having worked with Eric before on *The Dregs* and Ryan on *Headspace, Eternal* was a no-brainer. Great art and a special story in a size and genre I've never worked in before made this really exciting for me. Once pesky things like schedule and budget are sorted, I have a really good read of the script. Here I'm taking note of settings, characters and any important plot elements that will need to be researched.

Usually this is a great opportunity to do a deep dive into things related to the book that you just wouldn't normally have reason to read about. With *Eternal,* it was Viking stories in all forms of media. A day re-reading *Northlanders,* a couple of episodes of *Vikings* and *Norsemen, The 13th Warrior, Beowulf, Pathfinder, Outlander* and of course *Eric the Viking.* Now don't get me wrong, I'm not sitting back taking it easy while I'm doing this research, I'm finishing off whatever project I'm on at that particular time, in this case it was *Redneck* #8. I try to schedule one book at a time - but I usually end up jumping between a few different projects over the same period. Such is comics.

I wanted to approach the colors on this in a different way to how I colored *The Dregs* - there didn't seem much point in rehashing the same style. I usually set myself some rules to try and adhere to on a new book, but I always break these rules within a few pages! Seeing as this book was a *bande desinee* I wanted to treat it a similar style to *Asterix* or *Tin Tin,* but in a sympathetic blend with Eric's art. So I decided on minimal rendering, no grads and no texture overlays. I find myself using textures as a crutch so it's always nice to try and work without them. Of course I broke the no texture rule in every page by adding a watercolor overlay to the sky! And then I broke the minimal rendering rule on any page with strong lighting or fire!

Eric is a great collaborator - he trusts me to do what I feel is right for a page - but sometimes he has ideas and I trust his instincts as well. There's a wonderful sunset panel midway through the book that Eric sent me ref for. It was actually the first panel of the book I colored as I wanted to get a feel for the art and this helped set my vision for the book. I really wish this had been a spread or even a fancy art centerfold!

I spent a bit of time researching the kind of clothes Vikings and Picts would have worn and made a folder of lots of reference lifted from Google.

As expected there were lots of brown textiles, leather, furs and I threw a bit of woad blue in there too. Lagertha from *Vikings* essentially became my base model for Vif - Joan Bergin and the costume department for *Vikings* had done so much great research already. But the not-so-secret tip is that Google image search is your friend for researching reference!

The first stage of the actual coloring process is flatting the pages. Flatting is separating the art into flat, solid blocks of color which can then be easily selected when rendering the page. It is a time-consuming process that most professional colorists farm out. I started my comics career flatting pages for colorists like Len O'Grady, Lee Loughridge, Matt Wilson, Dave McCaig and dozens more.

It started as a hobby and soon became a full-time job, and in fact when the opportunity to flat *Sandman Overture* for Dave Stewart came about I actually quit my day job! It was probably one of my toughest gigs but I loved every page I did (I even got a name check in the hard cover edition - dream come true!). I still flat books for Lee and Matt and a few other colorists - it's a great opportunity to work on top titles that I wouldn't get a chance to based on my own

talents. But it's also actually a great learning process for me - I can play with color palettes as I'm flatting and then when I see what the actual colorist does I can see how to improve my own work. My flats for other colorists are in no way influential to their color process - they're just a good starting point! (While most colorists prefer if I supply them with 'clown' colors, I still use these pages as an opportunity to test palettes but I play with the hue/saturation slider before I send them on to the colorist so my choices have no influence on the final art.)

Other colorists prefer if I supply flats that are local color - sky is blue, grass is green, etc. And in some cases - like with Matt Wilson, who I've done probably 5000+ pages for - I like to try and color match scenes from previous books.

After the flats are complete I can start rendering the final colors. I don't necessarily make any color decisions on my flats, but it's a good place to start my thought process. Personally I try to work through scenes as opposed to chronologically. So if there are a set of pages that are all the same scene, I'll do them all in a row.

I approach all books differently, with completely different color choices, different rendering styles, even different brushes. Sometimes it can be a bit of a brain melt trying to remember how I treated one book if I've just come off another, but I tend to have a couple of go to brushes (and they're Kyle Webster brushes of course!).

As you'd expect, the art style very much determines how I approach a book. If the lines are loose it means my rendering can be loose. If the inks are bold and tight I can go for a more flat style or a cut and grad. It's really just a case of finding a sympathetic style of coloring that adds to the inks in each individual case. Some times I can see in my mind's eye how I would like the final page to look but have difficulty reproducing this on the final page, someone once told me this happens just before you level-up skills-wise, your hands just can't catch up with your brain! I'm a very literal colorist and I have complete envy over colorists who can do crazy colors but still make it look ace!

Most of the pages were set in snowy scenes, so having already decided how they would look I ran through all of those pages in one block.

That left a few other scenes to deal with, and in particular the wonderful page showing pastoral scenes changing through out the year. I really enjoyed the challenge of showing time passing. Again, Google was my friend - there were actually pages I found with photos showing the same location captured over the different seasons, which helped me choose a good palette.

I spotted an Icelandic word the other day: skammdegisskuggar. It's shadows of the short days; metaphorically, the darkness that can be cast into both land and spirit by deep winter. I think that perfectly encapsulates the feeling I was trying to achieve with Vif's journey into the Underworld. I really wanted to relay a completely different feeling to the rest of the book.

Knowing when a page is finished is a bit of a struggle, but having deadlines and multiple projects on the go kind of dictates when you need to leave it. I time pages by the amount of episodes of a show I watch on Netflix while I'm coloring them - I try to flat for one episode and then color over the course of another two or three. Like most artists in comics, I tend to not be a big fan of the work I've done for a considerable time afterwards, there's always the feeling that I should have spent a bit more time on it, or have done things slightly differently. But, after a few months have passed, I can look back fondly.

Ultimately, while every book is different, they all tend to follow the same process: read the script, research, flatting, render and FX.

I'm still not all that confident in my abilities and keep thinking I'm going to be caught out as an imposter, but I'm consistently offered fun projects with amazing creators, so there must be some method to the madness. The best thing is just to go for it!

eric zawadzki

is a Calgary based comic artist. He spends most of his time in the creator owned arena of the comic industry. As well as *ETERNAL*, he has co-created *THE DREGS, THE GHOST ENGINE, LAST BORN* and *HEADSPACE*.

Twitter: @ericxyz

ryan k lindsay

writes comics.

He has partnered with artist Eric Zawadzki to produce: *ETERNAL* through Black Mask Studios, and *HEADSPACE* with Sebastian Piriz through Monkeybrain Comics/ IDW.

He has partnered with artist Sami Kivelä to produce: *BEAUTIFUL CANVAS* through Black Mask Studios, *DEER EDITOR* through his own 'Four Colour Ray Gun' imprint and a handful of Kickstarter successes, and *CHUM* from ComixTribe.

He was selected as a participant in the DC Writing Workshop group of 2016.

His other comics include: Aurealis and Ledger Award winning *NEGATIVE SPACE* with Owen Gieni through Dark Horse Comics, *GLOVES* with Tommy Lee Edwards in the Vertigo CMYK anthology, as well as *EIR* with Alfie Gallagher, *INK ISLAND* with Craig Bruyn, and *STAIN THE SEAS SCARLET* with Alex Cormack through Kickstarter for 'Four Colour Ray Gun.'

He is Australian and when not being a family man he hones his writing skills by sacrificing blood wombats to the outback spider fight clubs.

dee cunniffe

is an award winning designer who worked for over a decade in publishing and advertising. He gave it all up to pursue his love of comics. He has worked for nearly every comic for every publisher as a flatter/color assistant to some of the world's top color artists. He currently colors as much as he can and someday hopes to be good at it!

Twitter: @deezoid

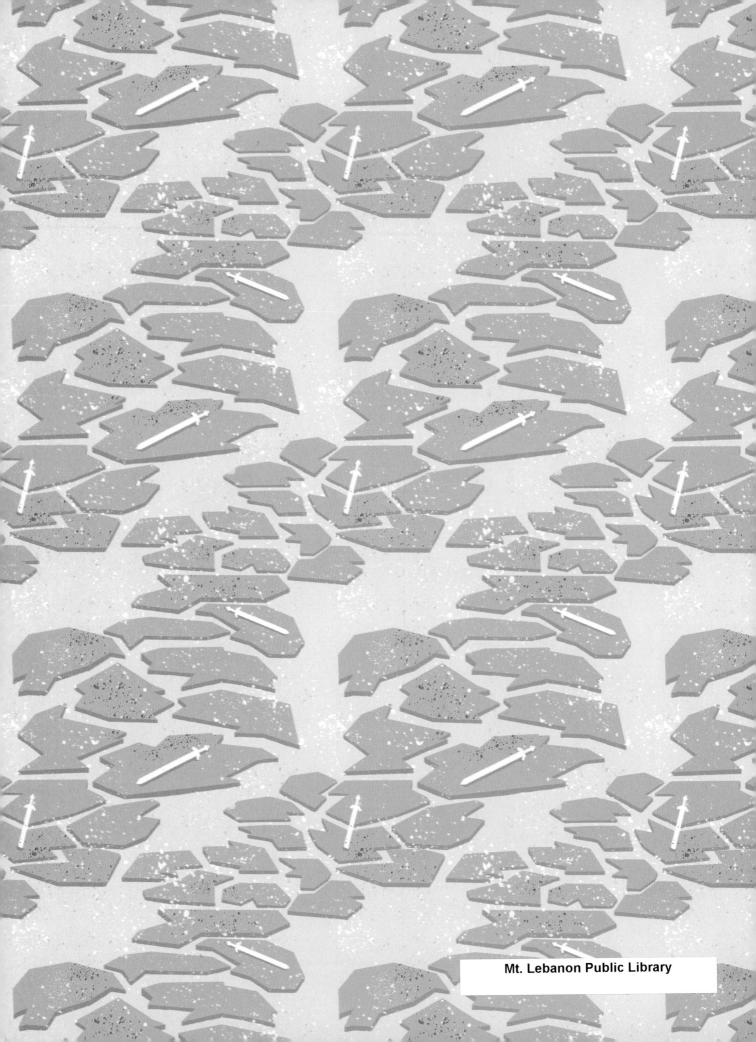